I0137401

Sable

and
Selected Poems

Sable

and

Selected Poems

Allan Johnston

SHANTI ARTS PUBLISHING
BRUNSWICK, MAINE

Sable and Selected Poems

Copyright © 2022 Allen Johnston

All Rights Reserved
No part of this document may be reproduced or
transmitted in any form or by any means without prior
written permission of the publisher, except in the case
of brief quotations embodied in critical reviews.

Published by Shanti Arts Publishing
Designed by Shanti Arts Designs

Cover image by FotoDuets on istockphoto.com / 838545534

Shanti Arts LLC
193 Hillside Road
Brunswick, Maine 04011
shantiarts.com

Printed in the United States of America

ISBN: 978-1-956056-53-2 (softcover)

Library of Congress Control Number: 2022943230

for Guillemette, forever

Contents

from Contingencies

from In a Window

Acknowledgments

These poems first appeared in the following journals, sometimes in different form:

Androgyne: "Clouds Crossing the San Francisco Bay"; *Argestes:* "Cutting Cedar Shakes in the Aladdin Star Valley, 1975"; *Ariel:* "In a Window"; *Bacon Review:* "Matilde" and "Wild Solo"; Bloomsday 2012, 90th Anniversary of the publication of *Ulysses* (online): "Piers"; *California Quarterly:* "The Tasks of Survival"; *Dickinson Review:* "Departures" and "The Workshop"; *Eighty on the Eighties:* "In Memory of Abbie Hoffman"; *Evansville Review:* "Shell"; *Fogged Clarity:* "Gone Too Far near Singing"; *Foxtail:* "The Witness"; *Jabberwock Review:* "Leaving Phoenix" from "Return"; *Lazy Bones Review:* "Octopus"; *The Literary Bohemian:* "Grape Cluster"; *Melusine:* "Contingencies"; *Mid-American Poetry Review:* "Hard"; *Midwest Quarterly:* "Entering Strange Cities"; *Modern Review:* "War Is Opened"; *New Verse News:* "Extinction"; *Poetry:* "Evening Conversation" and "Pound to Joyce"; *Poetry East:* "Meditation on Bliss" and "Visiting Grandmother"; *Poetry South:* "Stephenson Bridge Road" from "Return"; *QRLS:* "Climbing Blue Canyon, Lake Berryessa, California" from "Return"; *Rattle:* "Goats" and "Waitress"; *Redstart Plus:* "Five Explanations for the Moon"; *Rhino:* "Childhood near Hollywood" and "Potato Farming Near George, Washington, 1975"; *Rio:* "The Eater of Avocados"; *Seattle Review:* "Sable"; *Softblow:* "Old Town: Davis, California" from "Return"; *Verdad:* "Heard Singing"; *Visions International:* "Flight"; *Weber Studies:* "Beach," "Burning the Gas"; "Harvest," "Range of Light," and "Stars"; and from "Return": "Desolation," "Listening to Buddhists While Driving Into Nevada," "Mt. Tallac," "Red Duff," "Tahoe City," and "Tourists,"

Reprints of some of these poems also appeared in *Chiron Review, Ginosko, Interface, New Press Literary Quarterly, Strong Coffee, Third Lung Review,* and *Tipton Poetry Journal.*

"Hard" appeared in the 2010 TallGrass Writers' Guild anthology *Seasons of Change*, edited by Whitney Scott. Dyer, Indiana: Outrider Press, 2010, and won first prize in poetry for that anthology.

These poems were first published in the following collections:

Tasks of Survival: Selected Poems, 1970–1990. Lewiston, New York: Mellen Poetry Press, 1996.

Northport (Chapbook). Georgetown, Kentucky: Finishing Line Press, 2010.

Departures (Chapbook). Georgetown, Kentucky: Finishing Line Press, 2013.

Contingencies (Chapbook). Georgetown, Kentucky: Finishing Line Press, 2015.

In a Window. Brunswick, Maine: Shanti Arts Publishing, 2018.

The Illinois Arts Council provided a fellowship that supported work on "Sable."

Sable

Sable

The Sable Muse,
Being
The Life of the Negro Poetess *Phillis Peters,*
Née *Wheatley*, after the Name of her onetime Owners,
Written by *Herself,*
In a State of *Delirium,*
And included in a *Letter* Sent
By the *Authoress* Near the *End* of *Her Life*
And Heretofore *Lost*

NOTE: This fragment of a letter, from a bundle of documents saved from the house wherein the author died, remains one of the last testaments of her life, when, cast free from the loving hand of her owners, she sought to support herself in writing and teaching the rudiments thereof to the persons of her race; but being therein deceived of the values affixed to such services, and left at the hands of her wanton and sometimes unaccountable husband, was reduced to poverty, and her color being such as to deny her all employ but that which she abhorr'd, brought in a few short years thereafter her death, thus speaking of God's great Wisdom and Justice, that fate bespeak the condition it begs for.

You propose my returning to Africa with Bristol
Yamma and John Quamin...; but why do you hon'd
sir, wish those poor men so much trouble as to carry
me so long a voyage? Upon my arrival, how like a
Barbarian shou'd I look to the Natives; I can promise
that my tongue shall be quiet/for a strong reason
indeed/being an utter stranger to the language of
Anamaboe...

—Letter from Phillis Wheatley to
Sir John Thornton, 30 October 1774

'Twas mercy brought me from my Pagan land,
Taught my benighted soul to understand
That there's a God, that there's a Saviour too:
Once I redemption neither sought nor knew.

Your most obedient servant,

p.p.
p.s.:

I thank you once again for your inquiry
into my health. Sir, it now pleases God
to castigate me with the righteous rod
of constant illness. I await a birth.
I fear the best that God will now require me
to bear is time and child. What Our Lord's earth

may soon receive, I know. God's work is fate
for womankind, and brings her, for her pains,
the solace of the grave. I am past gains
from these and other turns. This life of gall,
the asthma and the heat of fevers late
encroaching on me, swells the seat of all

intense imaginings, and sets me loose
too often in delirium, or swings
me off from all constraint, to view such things
as summon my whole Life here, all anew,
to be discovered. What the point or use
of publication now is seems past view;

not mentioning the never-ending need
of drumming up subscriptions. Though creation
itself is ever beyond reprobation,
all such endeavor, without sponsorship,
seems without point. Still, as before, I heed
the muse in my reply to you. I skip

grand niceties, for, Sir, I'm to be made
laid open to the graces of God's pleasure
that fills me with this sickness as a measure
of my own sinfulness, whence only death
may waken me, unless some small cascade
of blessing pass down to me from God's breath

and lead me to continue. And it seems
th'effect is such that fevered *memories*
in mix with rambling *folly*, and with seas
of sad *remorse*, or *Fantasy*, o'erthrow
my weak estate. But oh, when flesh's schemes
and heart do fail me, may I come to know

my God, my strength and lot! May *Confidence*
still rest in high *Salvation*, the blessed part
of those who seek Him with the fullest heart!
        Your other proposition, which I weigh
with import still, and taste the consequence
it bears should I recover, if I may,

of my return to Africa (if so
it may yet ever be) with Omo and
John Quamin; why, Sir, do you still demand
that these poor men should bear the pall of trouble
that it would bring to ply my lot of woe
on voyage with them there? Would not this double

the burdens that they carry? Besides, on
arriving thence, how awkward would I seem
to *Natives* there; I fear that they would deem
that I myself am Barbarous. My tongue
would be mute by strong right, and I would fawn
in stupid shows of dumbness, for among

such natives I could never speak, the talk
now being lost to me. As for their plight—
their need of aid in turning to the light
and finding *Christ*, to work the great conversion
and sweetly bléssed saving of these folk
of *Africa*—Sir, I think that your version

of these events does little to conjure
my posture on imparting such sweet ration—
the place to which I feel that, by my station,
I am beholden, even while ('tis true)
I might be able to provide a sure
and able fitness suited to renew

its complement and fulfill its expansion.
I ask, instead, you bear in mind my fate,
and ask how I'd endure it.
                              I did wait
that day in Boston, for what *Providence*
had given me, and had as sole possession
a scrap of carpet, filthy, full of rents,

I'd found amidst the rubbish on the ship
to break the cold and offer some respite
from hacking breathlessness. Above, the light
of day was making gestures toward warming
despite the cold, and masts about did dip
above the frigates, like some massed and swarming

epiphany of gallows, with the steady
and rhythmic undulation where the wash
of *Charles's* River meets the inward rush
of tides. I watched the dock hands lead away
the "cargo," as they called them, and the ready
appliance of the whip and stick to pay

the line into the hut. And still the stench
was lingering: the reek of death remained,
persistent as the gulls that teased the wind.
I stayed among the mortal, wretched ill
as if of little value while the drench
of sweat from fever soaked the rug. And still

I thought how pointless it now was to plot
escape or flight; the sea, invincible
and capped with foam, now formed a mighty wall
more terrible than any I'd foreseen.
        I do confess, despite my soul's sad lot
and to eternal shame, my thoughts did lean

to means of my own death—a brooding spent
upon the way the swirling water chilled
the bones of all who in her had fulfilled
their destiny—the lucky ones—and those,
who borne aboard with child did thus relent
to desperation, and toss to the throes

of water in our wake their tiny bundles.
Barbarian indeed such cruel ends;
God only knows what justice this defends.
Barbarian, too, though, I, then, unenlightened
to such fine graciousness as Our Lord kindles
within our sinful hearts. If you are heightened

in your inquiry, Sir, once you have read
this letter, whence my thoughts have sprung, whence hopes
for common good still with resistance gropes
in taking up the missionary call,
remember: I, by seeming cruel thread
of fate, myself was snatched away from all

I'd ever known; from *Africa*, the heart
of all imagined childhood hopes and fears:
what pangs excruciating and mad fears
must there have burnt my mother, made her wild?
What steely soul, untouched by all her hurt,
could from such home have seized the loving child?

Such was my fate. But as the unchained souls
were forced within, the foetid cargo passed;
the salt taste of the harbored sea amassed,
and I, like one removed, swayed between death
and slavery, the land and water, walls.
I still rehearse that day, e'en now, as breath

seems to abate; see other, distant things
as should have been by will of prayer long since
erased, forgotten—family prayers, a prince,
the water poured to bless *Aurora's* glowing,
the fields and trees, the way the deep green sings,
the happy sons of vegetation growing

and spreading leaf in banner to the skies:
the mighty works of *Providence* we trace
in trees and plants and all the flowery race....
      I would have died to return to a home,
yet home now seemed as tenuous as the sighs
exhaled in all our weeks at sea, a sum

of passages past human reckoning.
I knew I'd never touch that distant shore,
and knew that somehow, even in that hour,
it came beneath the mantle of a dream—
a strange, evoked consistency of thing
like that which marks our lot since Satan's scheme

brought Adam's fall in penance for the sin
we all inherit. I'd learned words by chance
from red-faced sailors. As I looked against
the harbor's mouth, a peace or deadness seemed
to fall upon on me, and I peered within
with no intensity; perhaps I dreamed

upon the face of life's catastrophe,
the dance of human cruelty. Near the water,
where ships lay with their sails furled or aflutter,
I saw the walking couples, children playing
on bales of strange materials, a sea
of odd and dull-hued flows of dress outpaying

from garments so unlike the dress I'd known
in dreams of former life. Their darkened shade
set off the pallid skin. The town was splayed
behind the wharf, and plied with smoke, the dull
gray buildings belching soot and noise. The drone
of clanging sounds from iron mongers fell

upon my ears, a noise familiar
in some ways from my village. And did find
that some of us (I mean, of course, my kind)
were working in the vessels. How I got
up to the fence that bordered on the pier
and stretched out to our mooring, being so wrought

with my disease, I do not know. And yet
while all moved through the hut, now full of noise,
I leaned against the fence, watching the poise
of pylons as the sluggish waves played by,
revealing barnacles and starfish set
upon the sodden wood.

           I know not why
that couple did advance to look at me.
I moved back, having learned in innocence
the cruelty, the deep inheritance
so easily brought forth, the means and skill
that *Sin* partakes of in its rising spree
through chance to action—openings that kill

through pleasure, devil's work, to which no race
or cipher verifies dominion.
The torture of another oft seems spun
from whim, as with those seamen, who, to gain
more flavor of their mastery, would place
salt on the chafes and gashes of the chain

to magnify the howls of men below
within that ship. There are such horrid sights
that few I know have seen, or have by rights
admitted to, the *Gospel* having shown
the darkness of our lot, and let us know
the soul's corruption, for which we atone;

and we have also heard the explanation
how higher grace, made manifest in skin,
provides the evocation of *God's* plan.
And yet by chance we've also heard professed
the claimed equality of all men, kin
within dear, loving *Nature's* noble breast;

and if they take this just and noble plot
as matter of the household, those we serve
will recognize the weakness and reserve
of my own sex ... And yet I here digress.
I have the fear that sickness plays its lot
of fantasies, and that such dangers press

as winters bear in my condition ...
            I backed away—I could not face the chance
of cruelty—though now, with backward glance,
I count myself as blessed, to have them choose
to save me from the fate or sad perdition
that children suffer from those who abuse—

I backed away, and yet the old man's look
was neither hostile nor indifferent.
I now recall a face of good intent.
His sideburns seemed the fur off some coarse goat—
this I recall as the first thought that took
my fancy, looking on him there. His coat

of green-gold cloth had small brass buttons gleaming
upon the cuff. A sailor spoke that flow
of cacophonic sounds I'd come to know
as English. He made gestures at me, and
the man withdrew to speak to him. Then, seeming
to move out from behind, as by command,

the woman first appeared—my savior,
my dear, dear friend: pink-faced, thin, and quite frail,
so delicate atop the buoyant sail
of skirt she floated in, with small white lace
upon a blue-gray bodice clasped to collar
beneath her chin. I still think of the face

I must have made as I did in amazement
look on her there, for then she seemed afloat
on bubbling, rustling fabric, as without
her legs—just an upper part of torso,
the rest a sighing, billowing ruffle, meant
to hide beneath. This all amazed me so,

I moved to touch the cloth. The sailor's curse
was followed by his fist. Quick words were passed
between the men. The sailor, now aghast
with some appalled respect, relented. Fate
thus first showed me the man who would reverse
my fortune through my purchase. He'd relate

his version of this story as a staple
within the house. He would repeat it both
in solitude and company; in truth,
at moments when the house might seem to be
a family, and other times, at table,
as jest or sport, to dinner company

while I would stand behind my mistress's chair,
ready to serve or be a spectacle.
That day's events are too much to recall.
Just be it said I passed the gate and came,
half starved and wracked by asthmas, in their care.
They cajoled me and coaxed me, without shame,

through Boston's streets, the rope around me jerking
against my waist, stark naked.
                                                As I grew
it all became familiar: how smoke flew
from smitheries, the dark, loud, smelly toiling
so different from the open silver working
I'd known within my village, and the boiling

indecencies of taverns near the water,
the bustling people at each open stall
in markets strangely like those I recall
in that dream world I've come to know as other,
my home before enslavement, before capture,
and yet so different: grayish, dull-hued weather

of winter unlike anything I'd seen.
The summers only sometimes seemed to share
the brightness of that distant life elsewhere.
The governor's mansion: massive brickwork, tall,
with windows trimmed in white; the commons green,
my new home. God had saved me. That is all.

At times the house seemed more than home to me.
I slowly came to know that suffering
has meaning, and that some vast, greater thing—
God's *reasoning*, His high *beneficence*—
were manifest in my captivity,
my seizure from benighted innocence,

the sleep of all the world I once called home.
I still recall a day before the fire.
I dreamed about my brothers and the pyre
the family built to cook a suckling pig
in open air—the two, entwining, shone,
the one among the trees, and this one, big

within its box of brick, inside this room
on days when winter's winds would intercept
the life-limit of man. My mind was kept
ablaze between the comfort of past times,
this comfort of the present, crudely groomed
from inhospitable, unpleasant climes,

and those harsh fires that burned through my existence
in prayer and sermon, telling us our joy
in anything on earth becomes a toy
if we forsake the *Lord's* ordained commands.
For long since had I gained good *Christian* guidance
and such instruction as the faith demands.

My master, as you know, soon had me bent
unto the righteous path, as such was key
to my redemption and preparing me
for freedom in the house, whence I was placed
as part design behind my procurement.
For, as he often said, he had no taste

for slavery as such; the rest, from whom
I soon was kept, were mere necessity,
and he thought ill of all commodity
that built upon the bondage of a few,
and deemed such institutions fit to doom
when racked against the best progressive view;

and that the status of the races seemed
self-proving, given common human life.
I too saw what he meant. Among the strife
of Boston streets on Market day, I'd see
the half-dressed copper savages who gleamed
in every kind of gaudy show, half free

in tribal nakedness. And mark the man
who worked in loading cargo, how this shape
most noble was; yet disadvantage gaped
through lack of proper dress. Yet for my part,
I dared to think my gifts showed some great plan—
as if a sign of wonder from *Christ's* heart,

a presence blessed by my escape from toil,
and so for me a sign that God's great grace
need not in every instance spurn my race
in this strange land. The fire glowed, and the steam
came singing from the kettle. With the boil,
I took it off and made the water stream

into the pot, then measured out the tea
for Master and his calling friends, for those
I served in life.
                              I did not know the close
exactitudes of any plan or border
that held me there, defined as property:
not free, but free; not free, by law, if order

or mandate were to be believed; brought to it
by suasion, as it were, by love, and yet
not family exactly—not a pet;
for instance of my skin was evidence
of my ensured removal from some conduit
of home that I ignored, as in defense

of someplace that seemed slipping off in sleep
to worlds confined to dreams. The waking world
cut off all realms of dreams. In sleep, I hurled
in *Africa*, perhaps; perhaps not. Still
I moved I know not how out of the deep
remoteness of my native speech, until

when staring at him with his kindly face,
while he, at table, offered up the sage
enchantment of the black print on the page
of some book, I would lightly just pronounce
a syllable: here, *EY*. And come to place
a figure of a woman with a flounce,

or what I thought a woman ere I found
the letter was an *A*. Or would be told
the linkage of the figures he had scrawled
with sound: my name, in fact, that they had taken
as keepsake of the slave ship. Joining sound
with sight, the creeping rapture of the spoken

as transcribed into writing came to light
in ways that now I labor to recall
with clarity—in that, the word is all.
Perhaps it seems to blossom from its own
dark continent. I soon could speak and write
with some fluidity, and little tone

of accent. I recall I scribbled once
the forms of certain letters on the wall
with dingy lumps of coal. If I recall,
their anger balanced 'gainst my childish pride
in what I'd written, and gave confidence
that somehow I had found what was denied,

a tool. No one could know me for myself,
for someone held enslaved, a prisoner,
were it not for my favor, face, demeanor.
And hence, perhaps, the interest I took in
the books my master had on his great shelf,
with leather bindings trimmed in gold. I soon

began to read, with some instruction, both
from my dear mistress and her brood, who came
to view me like a sister, and would aim
at getting me to read with them; but soon
I'd left them far behind, to tell the truth,
and had read all those books, and for a boon

wrote fluently. They all seemed quite perplexed
to learn my strides, as feeble as they were,
in *Latin*. It would not be long before
a had a tutor. Soon I gained a sense
of many verses from each ancient text,
and also glimpsed the frontiers of pretense,

that work in *false beliefs* that's still so free
within our time. So after I read verse—
for instance, that of *Pope*—I could converse
through names of *Gods* and *Goddesses* that roamed
beneath the measured sensibility
of verses in my dreams. And when I combed

my mistress' golden hair, and sometimes found
the faint, clear strands of gray, so like the snow
when marred by smoke, I thought upon the glow
of sunshine in those distant lands, and knew
the singing words of *Goddesses* that sound
within the verse I later wrote in lieu

of conversation, on a secret slate
I hid beneath the bed as if somehow
it were the law to me, and made a vow
to start the work of ages. Whence began
that quiet voice that spoke within, so great
in singing from, through, inside, and so ran

in ways beyond all measure to believe?
I lived in words. I'd sometimes mumble them,
as to myself in fixing up a hem,
while I prepared a bath, or helped restore
the cloth upon my lady's frazzled sleeve.
The words were fine; they made up their own chore;

were glamorous in pleasuring their share
of rhythm, and the meter that could fix
the seeming rule of fantasy, and mix
in measured freedom.
       One day I walked late
into the Commons to buy food; from there
I passed down where the great ships disgorge freight

of cotton on the docks, and slave and free
address the bales. While looking, I, nonplussed,
felt longings such as never are discussed
and turned away. A squadron of young men
in *Scholars'* robes, enraptured with the glee
of *Disputation*, passed me by, and then,

in marking their discussion of the good,
their high, excited thoughts, I felt a fire—
not just the flesh's cauldrons of desire,
though I was of an age for such to start,
begun in the great trial of womanhood—
but also hope and wish to be a part,

to join in sprightly discourse, almost losing
my knowledge of my station in this moment,
and so, perhaps, most strongly sensing foment
increased by longing. I'd addressed a song
to noble *Virtue*, earlier—soft musing
on *Virtue's* leading *Chastity* along,

and how we should attend as *Virtue's* servant,
and so engage ourselves with qualities
as will confine our blooming years. Of these
I'd been forewarned, against the quickened word
of flesh that pulls us slowly to relent
to wretched sinfulness, such as I'd heard

was practiced in the taverns I passed by.
I had before me of brave lads a sample
ennobled in the accolades most ample
of sacred *Nature*, and, more, by the *Word*
of *Revelation* given from most high
by *Book* and *Master*, even as is heard

from *Holy Scripture*, whence must ever come
our moral strength. I felt a voice within
commanding songs of praise for these brave men.
That evening, when all in the household slept,
I took to pen and ink. I had a space
in which I kept belongings. There I crept

in light of tallow, so to do my labor
on poems and disputations—on some lays
to our then King, for instance, meant to praise
repealing of the shipping act, and be
acknowledgment of his great gift and favor,
as such as could make any subject free,

and so and suddenly did in my heart
rebound a voice that spoke to Rome, to plead
against the state of bondage, to be freed
to pursue honest earning from one's lot.
That night beneath the lamp did I impart
these simple lines of verse, with ease somewhat,

though also with some labor. These I showed
unto my mistress, who did soon address
my master with such works, to thus impress
and entertain him. But once he had read
my words, he seemed in such an altered mood,
none followed when he left. It soon was said

that I should wait upon him in his room.
I entered, filled with no small trepidation.
I'd heard of cruelties fed by lesser ration
of insubordination than I find
in writing, and although I did assume
my mistress and my master to be kind,

somehow the vision lingered of the whip
I'd heard and seen at work, though such is rare
upon the Boston street. He stopped me there,
and thrust out in his hand from off his desk
some sheafs whereon I saw my penmanship.
"Is this your work alone?" he then did ask.

I could not then deny it—did not want to—
would not, although I knew that the reward
could be injurious. I gave accord
to his suspicions. He then looked on me
as if not certain what he saw. "And do
you know how strange it even is to be

a slave who writes, and one whose verses sing
with resonances such as these—such themes
in homage of antiquity? Such dreams?
Do you consign a meaning to the word?"
He waved at me the address to the King.
I looked askance at this, for well I heard

the voice in which I'd written—as a slave
appealing to his master to be freed,
though such like thoughts were worked in with a knead
of largesse offered to the honor'd King—
I knew the words held danger. And yet gave
due credit to the *Scholar's* right to sing,

given the high ability to trace
eternity, as shown by *Jesus*' bliss,
and also how I'd left behind th'abyss
of errors, an *Egyptian* gloom, and crossed
the ocean only through a just God's grace
who brought me from the kingdom of the lost,

through tribulations safe from that domain,
with others, for whom, now, t'improve their right
as here they stayed in *God's* eternal light
and the great blessing of the purity
of true salvation, need instruction, plain,
to know the road to true equality

that's offered in like measure everywhere
to all who recognize their sinfulness
and bow to Him. I answered, "I confess
to knowing the significance therein,
if this is what you mean, my Lord. If there
is any tale concealed behind the scene,

I've read of it but only know it partly."
My words were standard, like fine jewels, in case
in first delight the flaw should lose its trace
in brilliance. My master took his ease
to read again the verse, and then looked smartly
at me again. "And are there more of these?"

I talked about the boats, said that reflection
had come to me that evening, and my yearning
to write my feelings when, the day returning
in introspection, I thought to employ
a diary I kept for circumspection
and instances of insight. Secret joy

did dance within my heart, yet also fear
and longing, for I wished my words to move
into effect in ways I scarce could prove
as possible. He read, then looked at me
again, then read. "You must show me here
your efforts if you write," he stated. "See

that you bring me your copy books. 'Tis better
to have you learn it proper. For my part,
I'll lend my hand to it as to impart
more Latin, even Greek, if necessary.
Should time remain, and should your chores not fetter,
attend me in this chamber. I will carry

the burden of your betterment, awaken
such accruements of knowledge as shall fit
your need of learning. I shall settle it,
and give you word of times when it will be
most proper that your duties be forsaken,
so you can meet me here." Whereupon he

did raise a hand, as gesture of dispatching,
and turned again away. I left, my heart
still pounding in my chest, in equal part
from fear and joy.
                      My lessons came with rapture.
With wonderment I sought the great unlatching
of Latin conjugations, and to capture

the language of the Gods—for so it might
be called. I filled my verse with understanding
of *Rome's* heroic past, and *Christ's* demanding
allegiances, and all the new-found worth
of modern science. Of the moon's vast height,
the distance near-immeasurable of earth

from kindly sun, *God's* chosen means to bless
and animate us all, I soon well knew:
the hunger of the sacraments came too,
for soon a sage advisor on such things
would join my other tutors, to compress
such clarifyings into reckonings

as would pertain to spirit and effect
our human sinfulness, the *Mark of Cain*.
My counselor did explicate the stain
all humans bear, the flood, the separation
of peoples of the earth, and the *Elect*
to whom God would show mercy. The creation

of differing hues; the children of *Elam*,
and *Ham*, and *Shem*; how skin reveals the trace
of sin in lines of color, and the race
of sons of *Israel* of varied clan,
and how, by suffering like a *Sacred Lamb*,
our Lord ensured the benefit of man—

by such means all the races could be whitened,
and thus redeemed for eternal salvation.
Though not of English stock, not of a nation
most pure in root, but just another child
of those lost Southern races, once enlightened,
by *God's grace* I could leave my once-beguiled

condition, and, my soul now purged of sin
I'd spin before dear Jesus in the light
that bleaches each race captured in this night
of earthly woes. Heart-felt obedience
alone could conjure God's grace, bear me in
to everlasting glory. Thus, the sense

and firm appeals to basic understanding
of the clarity of paradise
were shown to me, in ways that could suffice
in moments of my daily meditation
to illustrate how sin's perverse commanding
had cast me, *Ethiope*, from God's salvation;

thus God had sought to save me in my blackness
in this odd sea of white. Yet it would chance
that I would question this unswerving stance
as somehow quite interpretive: for I,
in looking on the heavens, could track less
of white than black in the enscriptur'd sky,

and saw how few the lights are and how faint,
and so did question in my sin the bent
of this white metaphor of God—well meant,
of course, yet somehow slant. Yet I did dread
to entertain such thought, for fear such taint
would hide me from God's grace. In all I read

and heard, Christ's gift had reason upon reason;
if ever any argument seemed feeble,
it was supported by the blessed *Bible*—
that vast reserve of blood, the crucifixion,
the miracle of suffering salvation,
and so seemed joined in ways to my affliction;

I thought my sin-stained soul might be received
in heaven. "Blesséd art those," Christ has said,
and dear and stark repentance have I made
for sins beyond my own. I know my race;
my life, my world are fixed somehow, relieved.
Such knowledge, now it strikes me, came apace

with my first elegy. A man collapsed
on Market Street one day while he was choking
upon some fish bones. His death was quite shocking
and very swift. The doctor came and went,
and I gave aid such as I could, yet lapsed
in helping ease the family's lament,

and by chance later stood beside the corpse
within the house, transfixed with sin, and rigid
with fixity of purpose in the frigid
and final selfishness of death. Such thought
reminded me of how such silence warps
the assurance that anguished suff'ring wrought

unto all questioning souls; e'en such as this,
a wax-faced, goutish walrus of a man
who lay here on the table by a pan
while I brought vessels full of water boiled
for cleansing of the body. I did guess
how others might have judged the scene: the moiled

and self-effacing *Negress* who'd been sent
among refined and cultured gentlemen
who came to bear the rights and regimen
of some vast blessing. She'd retell the pain
of vagrant sins cast long before Christ rent
the veil of sinfulness, and so explain

the freedom of the soul that lived within
the colored monument of flesh. Salvation,
in such a case, was death. I knew the station
upon the cross could lead to some green flowers
that blossomed in a now-lost world; the plain
simplicity of houses, place, bowers

I once had known. I turned to God.
                              I need
not tell you of those other men who gave
instruction: the first, regular and brave,
my tutor in the Bible, and the latter
more intermittent, teaching when he stayed
to visit at the household and to gather

all Boston as he did his circuits of
the colonies. These, with my family,
provided holy guidance. I could see
how their position could endorse *God's* way
in my enslavement; soon, too, saw the love
that acted underneath the textured play

of human acts. A new society
seemed being born about us, with the call
to *Nature's* guarantee of rights for *all*
expressed by the more strident pamphleteers,
and broadsides sent against the ubiquity
of regal impositions—brigadiers

now stationed in the houses, rights denied
to voicings on elections and taxation.
My counselors, concerned with my elation
and quick support of such rebellious cause,
maintained such actions countered the *King's pride*
and *God-sent* right as set forth in the laws.

Yet now did friends and counselors promote
my avocation. They had come to know
the rapid ease with which the verse could flow,
as sometimes when we had a dinner guest
who was surprised with something that I wrote
upon a tale just told. I was impressed

by acts of boldness or most happy fate.
Sometimes I'd write before them, every line
brought to a clever coupling that would shine
with wit. And now acquaintances would bring
the topics they would like me to relate
in poesy, to which end I would fling

my energies, and so give explication
to *Fancy's* role, or *Reason's* grave import,
or how these two live only as *Love's* sport.
I read aloud from these, and was commended
on my accomplishment, and approbation
supported me with compliments extended

and words of understanding, if not awe.
My gift, it seemed, though it may be a sin
to boast of such, would often let me spin
a poem on any subject that did suit
t'express the sympathy or blesséd law
of God, or else God's greatest gift, the fruit

of vast *Imagination*, now set free
in flows of Fancy borne by Love divine.
Whatever seemed to purpose would I line,
then copy and with grace dispose each time
a guest showed pleasure at the Muse's spree,
the more admired for rising from the rhyme

of a young *African*, and e'en a girl.
With such a gift, it was not long before
my fame in town advanced beyond our door
and people in the market might give smile
or nod, or even drop a precious pearl
of word, though always with a certain guile

in light of all the proper barricades
of status and of race that they perceived
and so preserved; and some, it seemed, received
an insult merely by my sight in ways
I had not sensed before; strange accolades
and grand elations of the blood in sprays

of epithet that hissed upon my passing,
which now I knew were clearly meant for me,
though said in such a way that each could be
denied in full to such a source as this
hard derogation. If my pride was massing
within my heart, it was to help dismiss

what I perceived as incandescent hatred
splashed from a feared inferiority
that stirred beneath it like a sloshing sea
upon a churning ship's bow. Strange to say
th'elation of those days was unabated,
just as, throughout the colonies, the spray

and heat of hatching revolution seemed
to blossom in the broadsides. And then there
was news of soldiers shooting in the square,
where murder'd was one whom I knew by name,
a servant to a family friend. I dreamed
that night of great Columbia.

                               My fame
grew with my writing, grew with the unrest.
For everywhere the voice of freedom sounded:
the breaking down of tyranny expounded;
now all possessed unalienable *rights*
by dint of *Nature* and its *God*, who blessed
and adjured all to join such noble fights

as seemed afoot. My counselor requested
I study how God works his will through all.
So when a famous orator did fall
in death's firm grasp, I felt my spirit bound
to composition, wrote on how death wrested
his soul from suffering, and how he found

the way to liberate us to the sense
of God's most wond'rous works. It seems to me
that I now worked in endless elegy,
my writing all pursuant to that vein,
though certain works I held against appearance
as bearing on the troubles that did strain

among the populations, or advance
too close to causes bearing on my plight,
and that of my black brethren, to see light.
And so my writing touched that liberty
that *God* may offer us in each *death's* chance
to rise among the angels and be free

from bondage which increasingly appeared
inimical to life. I did compose
in other veins, of course, and often chose
to offer works to print, and soon did court
the thought of having such works, well prepared,
within one tome. In this, I sought support

through patronage. Each counselor had his stance
upon this project, thinking of its source.
I contemplated th'advantages, of course,
that publishing might bring on me, as well
as any credit to my race, t'advance
the noble cause of any gradual

emancipation. My friends did promote
these lofty plans, and with that famous death
of our great orator, whose life and breath
and substance flowed from his great patron dame,
I thought to eulogize his passing, note
his value, and send copy to the same,

and so bring some attention to the plight
I faced with other *Africans*, here caught
in bonds of slavery, though theirs was not
relieved by love and approbation. Thus
I wrote an elegy which praised the light
of heaven brought within our grasp, for us

he honored, urging all *Americans*
to take the *Lord's* great *blessings* and to hold
the faith. And even to the slaves he told
the promises of *Jesus*, Who, *impartial*
in judgment even unto *Africans*
in His eternal wisdom, soon would marshal

both black and white within the ranks of *Priests*
and *Kings of His Great Realm.* I did address
a letter to his sponsor, whose distress
upon his swift departure from this life
was eased in how I told her that the feasts
of heaven now stood counter to her strife,

and how even a humble *African*
could share in her great mourning. This I sent
with my creation. You know how it went
thereafter—how her most gracious promotion
helped move my publication. In the span
of some few months this happened. The emotion

I found in having my work thus embraced
was only blemished by the hindrance
I had in finding someone who would chance
its taking on, and in the end the need
to have my hand in making it retraced
by those reputed of sufficient breed

or class to make report. And so one day
I sat in the town hall with my mistress
awaiting interview. The grave distress
it gave me was not slight, and yet I knew
the gifts I had from God, and so can say
I saw no need to shirk the rendezvous.

I soon was called, and shortly after came
into a room wherein a table ran
across the farther side. Each to a man
of these most noble *citizens* was seated
behind; I sat before. Each said his name
to clarify his function and repeated

a few words on the momentous intent
behind this episode—in short, to find
If I had proper qualities of mind
to write what I had written. There did sit
my master in the midst, to circumvent
such discourse as he thought might counterfeit

my qualities. God led me. The first spoke
to know about a passage that referred
to certain sections of *God's Holy Word*
as offered by the *Prophets*. I gave book,
chapter and verse, then someone did evoke
a parallel, as if he hoped to brook

no respite in my knowledge of each turn
in God's great message. I quoted the part;
in fact I know the Bible quite by heart,
and demonstrated how both texts unfold
redemption of the blessed while sinners burn
in fires of Hell. A third one then unrolled

his opulence. He was quite round, and red
within the face, and leaning on the table,
he asked me if I thought I would be able
to justify a reference derived
from *Pagan* sources. Answering, I said
that *Fashion* informs *Taste*, so I'd contrived

to study how the Poets mingle in
Aurora, *Phoebus*, and such deities
as in poetic diction serve to please
the reader, to support which I did name
the works of noble *Pope*, whose fancies spin
from such like chimeras of wit as fame

requires of poesy. I clarified
the meaning of such terms as I was asked,
then conjugated Latin verbs, and basked
in my ability to translate cold
a Latin passage given to decide
my strengths within this tongue. Then I was told

to wait outside. You know the facts related:
as witnessed by the most respected men
within the city, I could hold a pen
and write, and even though, at age of eight,
I was "*Barbarian*," "*uncultivated*,"
a "*Negro*" and a *Girl*, who bore the weight

or "*Disadvantage*" of the *African*,
and lived a slave within a family,
I showed a lively curiosity,
and without schooling past what was at hand
within my home, was reading like a man
in sixteen months, and so could understand

the hardest *Sacred* text, and also read
aloud to all's amazement and delight,
and in that span I also learned to write,
as witnessed by a letter I addressed
unto the *Indian's* minister, when he'd
embarked en route to London, and progressed

in Latin. That my works are such as may
be figured by the most respectable
to be by me, that I am capable,
and that the judges find fit to ensure
such qualities of genuine degree
as lead them to affix their signature

unto the document. My dearest thought
was that endorsement would increase the fame
of what I wrote, advance subscriptions, frame
the work for publication. Yet I found
that even such support as this was not
sufficient to erase the stigma crowned

by shade of skin. It was clear I'd not find
a voice within the colonies, and had
scant hope of bringing forth my book. Yet fad
or Fortune favored me; I was promoted
in *England*, where the patroness aligned
herself to my endeavor, and devoted

her energies in circles where my knack
and color held significance, and hence
assured that I would gain some recompense
for such abilities as indicate
the outrage slavery approbates, the attack
it makes on all just souls. I did not wait

too long to choose her favor. Adding in
the onslaughts of ongoing breathlessness
that often brought me to the brink of death
in childhood, and still threatened, it was thought
that journeying to England would begin
the process of my healing and be fraught

with opportunity for growth and gain
within the world of letters, where, to gauge
from what I heard, I was somewhat the rage
in reading circles. So, with my half-brother,
in five weeks' time I crossed the watery main
and disembarked, a new world to discover.

The opulence of *London!* Noble flavor
of elevated *Culture*, diverse toys
for each deserving soul whose brief hour joys
in taste of full distraction! It was there,
the few weeks of my stay, I came to savor
the great importance of a well-worked stare,

the finely disposed wit, stupendous wigs,
and free mobility of every sense.
The trip alone seemed perfect recompense
for any honor my work would avow:
the people that I met, the regal gigues
I danced, my fine reception, even how

the noble houses opened, granting meeting
with lords who kindly indisposed themselves
for half an hour's talk, or from their shelves
brought down the august volumes of the wits
or furnished me with coin to gain a seating
at some or other spectacle, as fits
the proper taste.

Five weeks of passage brought
me to that land. My young master came, too;
he kept nearby to guarantee I knew
and followed protocol, and to protect
me from all harm, but also to give thought
to any cares or cures he deemed correct

for health in general, as my condition
had wavered in those hectic months before
departure. With the letters that I bore
of introduction, I became perturbed
when my own patroness declined permission
to wait on her, and though I felt I curbed

my disappointment in my correspondence,
she must have sensed it when my letters claimed
that one who sought to have my image framed
within the frontispiece should easily
be able to acknowledge the despondence
such actions caused, and view reality

as present in the person. Nonetheless,
I showered onto her my heart-felt thanks
for her acceptance of me in her ranks
of patronage with humble dedication
to her within the volume, for the press
would never have accepted my creation

but for the gift of her support. As to
the circumstance of any criticism
descending from my color, witticism
alone could aid me there, and happenstance
that I be shielded partly from it through
my patronage. Meanwhile, my circumstance

insisted I be fêted here and there.
I met a great professor of the art
of *Rhetoric*, who to me did impart
his interest in my special gift, though since
I've wondered if he did not fully bare
his true intent and purpose, and so mince
his words with guiles of those great citizens

whose interest lay in finding out if I,
an *African*, could reach the noble sky
of oratory, seemingly reserved
for those of proper station. If the lens
through which I thus view London is well served

by anything, it would be this—the hint
of unexpressed intention in the way
a meeting is avoided, or a play
of words brings *double entendre,* here used
to satisfy the knowing, and prevent
all others from acceptance—the refused

who show the gift but lack the birth, who fail
the test of proper heritage. But still
those few weeks gave me matters that could fill
a life of expectation. I did see
as much as time permitted, and avail
myself of opportunity to be

an emblem of a system, gaily mixing
with Lords and Ladies. Even *Franklin* came
to see me. My half-brother felt some shame
at his contingency, with visitations
and being called upon so often fixing
such time as was my own with occupations.

       I met a man who'd sailed around the world
and published books on everything he'd seen.
He did not judge, but studied, and did lean
to favor *God's* sublime variety
in making *Mankind.* For him, slavery hurled
his people into darkness, bigotry,

and bleak abomination. He had fought
to gain sweet passage of the law that gave
dear *Freedom's* gift to each and every slave
who entered England, and urged me to stay
in *Freedom's* loving light, on which I thought,
and might well have concurred, had not the play

of fate brought news of my Lady's distress
and fast-approaching end. We did prepare
itineraries, pack goods, and book our fare
upon the ship next set to hoist its sails,
and were near leaving when my patroness
sent word that I should wait on her in Wales,

that she had met a *Black*, a man of gift
in something not so patently expressed.
I sent my thanks but vowed that I was pressed
to leave by circumstances past control.
I let her know my sorrow at this rift
which caused such consternation in my soul,

but stated that by duty I must act
to aid my dying mistress—she who'd wrought
such preparations for me as our lot
can ever offer in this veil of tears.
Throughout that hellish voyage I was racked
by hacking fits of fever. But our fears

proved groundless. Long before we could return
to Boston, my dear mistress had rebounded,
though death still hovered near. But I was hounded
by my own sickness now. Asthmatic hacking
devoured my health, and I would freeze and burn
in alternating fits. All which gave backing

to my enhanced awareness of how slight
our pains are when compared with *Christ's* dire pain,
and how, like Esau, I'd tried to attain
my sensual pleasure with my right of birth
within God's holy kingdom, where the light
of Christ will save those chosen from this earth

from deep, eternal misery.
                       The weight
of sickness lessened near the time I met
my husband first. A certain etiquette—
or caution—favored transport of some letters
in private from a dear friend whose estate,
at some remove from Boston, enforced fetters

on uncontrolled expression between servants
in any writing, virtuous though it be.
He brought a missive from this friend to me,
and thus I soon was conscript to his fate.
How could I then know how the turns of chance
would bring such love and duty, joy and weight?

I marked his presence in a letter sent
as answer to the one received, wherein
his dear solicitude as go between
was mentioned. He was noble in his carriage,
and in this unlike those whose measurement
of opportunity passed his. If marriage

appears discounted through such neutral comments,
it is volitional; hot starts of love
mislead us in our duty. For above
consideration of my joy and pain,
I held the *Christian* bundle of commitments
to those who'd rescued me from the dark stain

of ignorance of God's immortal light,
and so remained aloof. A sudden bloom
from chance acquaintance can well seal one's doom
and bind one to a man one knows but barely,
but such obsessions also can cast spite
onto relations one holds dear. Chance rarely

reveals true love beneath infatuation.
I forced him out of mind once I'd received
the letter. I'd been told how men deceived
once they'd abandoned bondage to the chain
of *righteous* faith. The sweet intoxication
I sensed in meeting him held such a stain

as might not ever wash away if left
to taint the cloth, the way the wound unheeded
corrupts the flesh. To say that something needed
to be expressed in me—to hold in favor
the way his eye would not turn from the cleft
that split hope from his chances—were to savor

the reason I held such a man at length—
to tell the truth, to coddle secretly
the sight of one who showed abundantly
the fire endowed with that great seed of light
I knew as liberty, and which by strength
alone seemed bent on reaching some vast height

despite all circumstance. I could expound,
and say that from this some curse forged the chain
of all the growing anger and the pain
I nourished as each jockeying attempt
to flourish fell prey to a world quite bound
to hold his rough endeavors in contempt,

undoing each chance through its drab denial
of fortune to our race; more damaging,
I fear, the sickened children I would bring
into this world to turn into the grave
in quick succession through the mortal trial
we all endure as Our Lord's great and brave

desire to make us bend unto *His* Law
to feed *His* glory. Only in this sense
can I equate those souls of innocence
He takes away from us with righteousness.
Thus if I say that when we met, I saw
a man who served as vehicle to press

acquaintance via letters that did pray
for news of my great voyage, and return
the same by said same vehicle, I yearn
not to deny that, later on, my heart
did open, and how, as you know, the day
of manumission passed, I took the part

of womanhood, and became wife. If I
had seen what would arise therefrom, would I
have skipped this noble route? I can't deny
that he would often slip in ventures quite
as near to subterfuge as any I
could compass. Subtle twists seemed to indict

each effort to gain foothold in this world
of inequality wherein he, *Black*,
could seldom find employment fit to back
his own endeavors, much less keep a wife.
And that this burden came as we were hurled
into the jaws of war made it more rife

with pain—the way we broke the frozen earth
to bury my small babies, whose gestations
did eat my health the way the undulations
upon the sea erode the looming bluff.
I died in stages each time I gave birth.
Can I say that I hold to be enough

all such relations as life brought to me?
It's wiser to acknowledge that the sorrow
of living never guarantees tomorrow
on earth, and that our duty is our fill:
we ascertain our liability
in living through the deaths of others. Still

for some few years we loved; it ended slowly,
and now in some ways seems quite incidental
to circumstance: the pain, the incremental
appurtenance of poverty, remorse
in births and deaths of children, all the lowly
efforts to find work, the hardened, coarse

endeavors that through years make one immured
to pain and hate and love.
                                        But I digress.
That year I nursed my mistress through distress.
She kept the spoiling sickness on the run,
yet never quite revived. I felt assured
that she would heal, yet dying had begun,

and by accretions gained on her. Her dying
encased the year. Each day, the wondrous change
of God's acceptance flowered in the range
and distance of her eyes. My thoughts returned
to *Africa*, where God's work lingered, crying
to be received, while here the country burned

with loathing, as it seemed, for God: for even
as war approached a savage atheism
besmirched sweet *Reason*, marking with a schism
the face of righteous anger that had grown
against the British forces, as if driven
by powers that pass the force of man or throne

or even the idea of liberty,
so hotly mentioned in the streets. The land
was rife with rebel sentiments; the hand
of *Reason* held up *Revelation's* claim
to God's *impartial* justice. I did see
my mistress change, too, under *Judgment's* flame,

which lit her in delight with the great form
of *Christ's* descent. So even as the world
knew Freedom's fervent spark, I myself hurled
into those moments of the utmost care
that slow death so demands. For months the storm
of dying simmered in her; then the flare

caressed her, and I thought how I, outcast,
a stranger when she took me in her heart
and offered me her guidance, seemed a part
of her own flesh descendant. My own health
was wracked throughout her dying, and at last
as she departed from this world, the wealth

of God's great mercy in receiving us
upon His cross of suffering did shine
upon her base affliction. May she mine
the treasures of celestial gold, and grow
with that eternal weight of heavenly bliss
and holiness that everywhere did glow

about her in her last hours in this life.
She called us to her bedside and did charge
that we not shirk the great work still at large,
but hold to God's commandment. Then she cried,
"Come quickly! Come! Oh, take me for Thy wife!"
and passed. I sat the whole time by her side

and saw with grief and wonder the effects
of sin upon humanity.
                                    My freeing
had been advanced some time before, but seeing
the need for hospice, I'd remained within
the household and performed such as reflects
upon my solemn duty to unpin

celestial grace. Quite soon then for my ease
The papers were in order, so no heir
within the house could count me as a share
or win me through a suit. Such property
as I was given came as paltry fees
for all my years of service, but could be

quite better measured by my care and feeding
and general sustenance. But with her death
the household changed. It seemed as if the breath
had been released from some long held-in sigh,
and with the breath released, what had been seeding
within burst forth as with an angry cry,

and swept us onward. My master maintained
that all rebellion against the Crown
was horrid *Treason*, and he'd often frown
upon my fervor for the *noble cause*
of great impartial *Freedom* to be gained
through provocations quite outside the laws,

and now he held that *God* made *Monarch* master
through sacred vows that certified his right
as shown by the investment of all might
unto him by *Our Lord*, and clearly proved
by how some rule while others slave. Disaster
would issue from rebellion. I was moved

to credit his concerns, yet those who cried
for liberty, and soon for separation,
bespoke my soul. I felt that if a nation
could form and hold equality for all,
it would be from the *Revolutionary* tide
brought forth by *Freedom's* strident, vigorous call.

And so my writing grew with the unrest.
For everywhere sweet liberty resounded,
the casting off of *tyranny* expounded,
and all accorded unalienable right
by dint of *Nature* and its *God*, which blessed
and adjured all to join force in the fight,

remove the threat thrust on our colonies.
Such heady times! How could I not be fused
to such a cause? A girl, a slave, one used;
brought to this land in ways too foul to tell,
left only with the faintest memories
of my own mother bowing at the well

to thank her gods for water, after warm
and sultry days; the happy rivers teeming
with such abundant life—I look back, seeming
to understand, and forward to the time
when, with my truest faith, the deepest swarm
of feeling in my soul, I can hear chime

the sacred bells of freedom, and so walk
as free among the men of each and all
the nations freed within the brilliant call
of revelation, reconciliation
among my people; I could not but talk
in seeing springtime's blush as demonstration,

and fix my hopes that priceless liberty
would conquer prejudice, as God is said
to come impartially unto the red,
or white or brown or black. As Revelation
is open to us all, enslaved and free,
so can equality approach each station,

eternal, open, free! The revolution
devoured my heart with hope, for soon all souls
would walk in Reason's light as it unrolls
beneath God's truth of universal grace
for all. My master's words made the solution
more evident. I soon found my own place.

My master died soon after that; his son,
and then the daughter, moved to England, so
I sought such work as I felt I could do
in my infirm condition. And now, free
of such responsibilities as none
but women know, I thought in ecstasy

of opening a school for my kind
to aid their moral strengthening! But found
the separation somehow cut the ground
beneath my feet; those whom I once had known
as friends in social settings now did mind
their tongues in passing me, and frowns were thrown

upon attempts at conversation even
to point of fear that I would be attacked
to pay for some servility I lacked
in speaking out so freely. I perceived
a plague-like meanness in some people, given
the general conditions they believed

distinguished me, a *free* and *married* soul,
from them. Such harsh awakenings resound;
our lives are rumbled, boiling wars, the sound
of which increases steadily. The red
of soldiers in bright uniforms would pull
the world this way still more. They oft were fed

quite willingly, but too often imposed
their martial law on any homes that were
to their desire, which practice caused a stir
of indignation heightened by the brawl
as each night all the public houses closed
with noisy soldiers barely fit to crawl

into the gutters where they sometimes slept
in drunken stupors. Soon the general air
of discontent was trembled with a flair
of insurrection as the anger rose
against these impositions. Passions leapt
out of such hearts as normally repose

in fevered public moments. All soon donned
a guise such as the credulous world knew
when years before the rebel-rousers threw
the tea into the harbor to express
their anger at taxation. And beyond,
the sense arose that one could not repress

the voice that threaded through the colony
the way a snake would thread luxurious coils
through grass. My journey undertaken, toils
released, my womb in yield, my mistress dead,
I now watched as the whole community
advanced into war's flames. Could I not dread

for all our fates? One family turned to ashes,
my thoughts of this land now were sweetly tempered
by recollection of a land remembered,
another woman bowing to the east
I'd once known as my mother—sudden flashes
of memory; perhaps of what I least

expected; recognition, recompense
emerging in the possibilities
that strengthened now within me, beyond trees
so far past hope all seemed now caught in dream—
a world around me bending out of sense
as time and circumstance fished to redeem

those thoughts and visions flowing out like water.
And yet a real possibility
appeared behind such words as liberty,
and justice seemed for these brief, filmy years
as palpable as clay touched by the potter
that takes its shape as each hand swoops and veers

to gently round out all deficiency
that marks the vessel of our lives. The war
erupted. Young lads lay shot, and the roar
of musketry, death's voice, filled each report
of slaughter—Lexington saw butchery,
and Concord suffered much the same. The port

fell quickly to the foe. Blockade and siege
succeeded. When the British came, the fight
was fierce. Our army fell back in the night,
and then began the firing of the town.
We fled the burning sections, but the rage
of smoke and flame was such to make us drown

in terrors marked by ecstasy. The world
ablaze—the yielding blockade! In the streets,
the stumbling fear-struck hindered all retreats
as hot confusion reigned. And when we woke
from this nightmare of riot, our lives hurled
into an order enjoined by the poke

of bayonets, harsh force. The garrison
increased in strength. The Lord Mayor built forts;
new ships arrived; the *Redcoats* clogged the ports;
the *Rule of Crown* returned. But now the dirt
of subjugation smeared each citizen,
for all lost chance and power to exert

such rights as any citizen should hold
except as British sanction might advance
some person's station through some happy chance,
or for his fawning cowardice. But then
the fray fell back upon us, for a fold
of hills near town became a rebel den,

and continental troops seized hilltops over
the garrison, and British troops advanced
into the pall of musket shot that danced
both past and through them. Cannon fire did rain
upon the town, and clouds of smoke did hover
upon the streets. As soldiers screamed with pain

a languor seized the townsmen, as to blur
the bloodbath from its place in conscious thought.
We heard the cannon and the musket shot
resounding in the distance, and the smoke
that drifted through the streets seemed like a slur
obliged by the malevolence that spoke

through all these horrid strokes of war. The air
was filled with puffy ciphers that snared all
they fettered, each amorphous in its scrawl,
each hostile in its message. War became
escape from time, lacuna. Soon our fair
dear Boston burned again—lives ruined, the game

of war's fierce hungers played on hungry times.
In secret I wrote odes and letters, dense
exploratory tests of words, intense
re-renderings of dear *Columbia*,
the ornament of *Liberty*, whose rhymes
foretold the freedom of *America*,

appealed to rights of man, equality—
such sounds as were expressed by men who seemed
predestined to fulfill all that they dreamed
through insurrection when this war began.
We now were drenched in blood, and would be free,
it seemed, in death—freed by the blood that ran

so red and rich from black and white man both.
In this invention of a new-found order
we saw revealed the truths of sacred Nature
and *Nature's God*, of *life* and *liberty*,
and *happiness*, and *union* as the oath
that bound the peoples of each colony.

The savage hope that held the hand of reason
and dispersed in the judgment of those years
the harsh effect of interposing fears
now weighed upon us constantly, for all
the difficulties of that time did season
my own support of liberty. I'd call

for insight and for learning from the one
ideal: the sight of liberty emblazoned
within a heaven called the future, reasoned
to be far better than the times we'd see
within this war. I only hoped to summon
whatever hope would let us finish free.

My marriage, you know, soon ensued, as said,
and so began that portion of my life
in which I maintained duties as a wife
while he whom I had married came and went,
alive with all the enterprise that fed
his dreaming. I kept my own duties, bent

on being mindful of his word, as it
is woman's ordained office to obey.
For some time we had rooms, but with the play
of fortune in those times, I'd lodge elsewhere
or live alone at times. If love's sweet profit
requires its object's presence for its share

of full or wholesome food, then we defiled
(though this word is too strong) the sanctity
that comes from union, and stayed somehow free
of that most deep-held bond. Each circumstance
demanded, even as I filled with child,
his oft-times long removal, on the chance

of some success or other. He seemed called
as far out in the world as he could go
without, in fact, being gone. And as you know
I suffered through it as the world collapsed
through that harsh war. In fact, sometimes, when galled
by hunger, I would seek what could be grasped

of any aid, and sought out any port
that I could harbor in. His interests grew,
but nearly all he earned was spent anew
on covenants of promised wealth. At first
I too believed, and felt that each report
of opportunity was near aburst

with golden paths to fortune. I was left
with what small means I had, and would implore
such friends as could to aid me as I bore
the weight of pregnancy. Of course it's not
intemperance that made him so bereft
of any sense that every chance he got

was not the door to what we both most needed:
security, not one more call to gain
respectability from any strain
of business that would bear a Black. I'd write
as chance allowed. But as each chance receded,
though staying dutiful, I thought, at night,

sometimes, alone, about how life had played.
I tried to gain assignments as would fit
domestic skills I held, for I could knit,
and sew or darn—such work brought in some wealth
while I served as his wife; him I obeyed;
yet soon my passions faded with my health,

and one day, while about to snip a hem,
I saw our marriage turned to an arrangement,
devoid of choice. I came to know estrangement,
and though I remained wife, knew where I stood.
I took in work, bore children, buried them,
and wrote in fragments every chance I could.

The ways we survived then—sometimes, amazed
and stupefied with hunger, I sought space
with a young black man left to mind the place
his owner had deserted in his flight
out of the city when it first was crazed
with "English fever." Later on, the light

of kindness came from elsewhere. An old friend
looked after us. We moved about a while.
The country side was ravished by the vile
ransacking of all rations by the troops
of either side, and food was scarce. I'd find
what fed us every day. Life came in scoops

of dry peas gathered here and there, clear water,
a few old rags to clothe us, and the hell
of harsh, remorseless winters. Like a shell
that no longer housed life, the joy and ease
we once had known lay fractured by the slaughter
and—what was worse—the pestilent disease

that even all the lime thrown on the slain
could not eliminate, for every house
was plagued by it, worse than the foe. A douse
of joy, my first child, ended when he fell
into the pangs of fever and, midst stain
of blood and vomit, passed. Through all that hell
We had to bury him amongst the graves

dug for the soldiers. Our lives seemed to veer
between explosions of the world with fear
and listless neediness that neared starvation.
My child had died; I too was close. Such powers
as ever shape the hard birth of a nation

I plunged into the odes I used to purge
the dread that seemed more numbing every hour.
The harsh and final grave now seemed to flower,
and prospered with each pregnancy that came
to sap my strength and empty me of urge
to live without the little ones I'd name

E'en as I buried them. Salvation's gleam
fills every death that brings us to begin
existence in a realm outside of sin
and misery, where all is new and more.
In such harsh years, with freest hope we dream
that all will be revisited before

the dire effects of war, the deprivation,
the scrounging after food wherever one could,
the bartering and selling of each good
for far below its value, all the pain
we suffered, clinging on, close to starvation,
the way we saw no virtue and no gain

of advantage in people who, corrupted,
beguiled the citizens with each alarm,
and my own sufferings, the breaking harm
of deaths as foul plagues tortured us no end,
my loss of my own children, the disrupted
effect on my own marriage, as my friend

and husband wandered far and wide for gain
to reach the point that he was coming home
less often than he was out on the roam
for opportunities supplied by war;
those sad abuses breaking through the pain
of all that we held in, sir, soon by far

outstripped all the supposed gain one found
in those bleak years. And yet I never waned
in showing my support for those who gained
their sometimes sorry victories, their losses
more painful as the British did confound
our knowledge with reports and endless bosses

of polish to the rhetoric of King
and Crown, of loyalty so-called, to bind
a hopelessness among us in the mind.
and so I wrote each chance I could, to give
support to all our efforts, everything
we stood for. If in those years all did live

from hand to mouth, from moment to next moment
on what one could, I managed still to scribe
a message to our leader, and imbibe
the muse in brave support of *Washington*,
who soon received my missive, and did front
his own reply to me, and thought to run

the rallying of troops through pamphleteering
of these meek rhymes. I sought to meet him, but
my efforts failed. I wrote from heart and gut,
for who'd acknowledge how this vast, great reign
of dear Columbia from profiteering
was suffering, and how, for all our pain,

establishment of true and noble *Commerce*
could represent the only noble end
for our own country when, each friend to friend,
we all shall benefit from that great wealth
our new-found nation promises? No worse
was all that I could do to maintain health

as I put missive after missive out
to post my poems in presses and to seek
support for a new opus that would streak
into the vast Elysium of thought,
the noble cause of freedom. Did I seek
beyond the possible, or was I caught,

betrayed by hope, held by my skin? For each
endeavor met with failure. Some would turn
me out with such invective as would spurn
the writings of a lowly Black, whose hope
was obviously beyond the tainted reach
of any gift that Nature would have scope

to place into her hands. So do I end.
Sick, dying, as it now appears, it seems
that everywhere the promise of my dreams
collapses in this cradle of harsh war,
this world in which I live without a friend,
this child I bear within me, as before;

the pains I have endured, the life I saw,
the sick bed and the great weight of this child
seem thinking to dismiss me. If the wild
revision of my life were now allowed,
would I be constant to the sacred Law
I learned here in this time? How would the crowd

of faces take it if, that day in youth,
in maidenhead, I had not been removed
unto this country? Would I still have proved
a noble soul, a poetess, the lamb
of God's great blessing? Would the sacred truth
have been revealed, or necessary? Can

I say without a doubt that all this pain
and love was for my benefit? Was bound
to carry me through seas of sight and sound
and suffering, to such a sacred shore
as this, the land where hope is all we gain,
a westward land where all that lies before

stands naked as a continent untamed,
a promise or a curse, a corpse, a dream?
May all affect us as we hope will seem
amenable for all blessings we gain
in God's salvation, memory so named
to be our epitaph. So I remain

Your most obedient servant,

from

Tasks of Survival

Five Explanations for the Moon

Wolf

I howled you out.
You caught between my
teeth. I spat
a long white O
of you into
the air. You try
to hide but I
still find you there.

Cloud

The monopod crawls from its shell
in the wet season; it leaves tracks
ringed in the silver of its sky.
Hidden water will fall on mountains.

Fit

I tried to forget you.
I put you in the vase,
inverted you,
tacked you up on my ceiling.
When the blood ran down your legs I panicked.
I climbed through the hole in the negative sky.

Work

All day the people forget about you.
All night the moths try to reach your face.

Mirror

When I open the mirror
a world spins off
to my right. I watch
the quick flash
of everything
as it flies away.
You dance on the crazy waves of the sea.

The Tasks of Survival

–after Van Gogh

There is a vast security
in all this, how the plains fall
away from everything, how fields of crops
nestle in tracts of dead grasses

owned, of course, but small white butterflies
rest upon alfalfa flowers
just for a moment, then lift, leave
through veils of insect voices, birdsong,
the faint buzz of a chain saw's motor
naming the tasks of survival.

The ancients knew these names once;
field fall before cities
in Books of Hours, and Brueghel's "Winter"
captures the hunters on fallen snow
forever, the village still distant, the warmth
of the home hearth unimaginable
as God. Slowed by their kill, they lunge
through snow drifts brown as octogenarian
skin, their thoughts not touching the breaking
paint, the cracked veneer of themselves
remote as the fire of another artist,
also Flemish, who slashed his canvas
with thick cuts of gold-yellow grass
and dense black stabs of departing birds.

He pulls the cord; the saw descants
in his hand; he lowers the bar to the bolt.
The sing and heat of the cut throws out
the yellow chips of the heartwood, pushes
the saw through as he leans on the handle
and barbs the spikes in the bark for grip
while the bolt bisects, rings wrought rough
with the tip of the metal, the rasping chain.

The Workshop

Evenings my father would climb he stairs
to his workshop, turn on the radio,
and sit down to his planes. I'd run
down the street, find Phil or Todd; we'd play
in the backyard with plastic soldiers
and snap-together tanks, fill the garden
with little furrows, tiny ditches
in which small men lay dead, their legs
held up in the air by plastic stands,
their sole means of support. My father
found other ways—balsa wood, paper, glue—
to hold his time together. His fingers
formed scaled miniatures
of the planes the aces flew
in the war to end all wars. Von Richtofen's
Fokker, Rickenbacker's Spad; each model
became a dream that he could whirl
on the ends of wires, propellers chopping
the air. In his workshop, preoccupied
with diagrams and pieces of wood,
his radio blaring muzak, he'd lose
the world of work and weapons, his devotion
of his life to our nation's defense,
his duty to his country, become
his own country, a land secured
by escadrilles of bi-planes flown
by noble and chivalrous sportsmen.
                    Darkness.
My friends gone home. TV or sleep.
Or both. Small bodies sprout
across the backyard, heir to the roar
of the stars, the gathering chill,
the music that floats from a small lit window.

Clouds Crossing the San Francisco Bay

                                                                  Still

they march across water   cousins of solidity
boatloads of refugees from some oceanic

war. They want to adapt   are forming
into interpretations of a tense,

past perfect   subjunctive
becoming strange statues
of arbitrary women who talk

of dropping blonde water on mountains. Caught
in the air, wind molded, they become familiar.

Don't you know that one? Wasn't that San Mateo,
1978? They are losing themselves

in water   obscuring the crenellations

of the city, itself a poor imitation
of clouds, too square,   the wrong shade of gray.

                    They will pass to the east.

            They will sweeten the fields.

The Witness

I am on the second floor up from the earth,
watching a yellow sky west itself
to sunrise; your eyes move
with visions of a second earth

where my ghost wanders the distances
the stars have set between us, or something moves
with the changing light or the sound of a car
passing in the street below.
                        It is morning;

I watch as you sleep. One hand
hangs in the air from the sheets like a pine bough
in a forest in rain. It is morning,
before sunrise and radio alarms,

and sleep is slowly lifting away,
lingering in hair and bone
like mist in fields where hunters move
dissipating slowly to

some cool, ceramic slip of sky
where stars shudder to nothingness
behind light that dawns on us,
eradicating heavens or dreams

paradisiacal
        promised respite
from some strange, fantastic hope
that wings us behind eyelids.
                        I am here
to watch you as you waken, to witness.

from

Northport

Potato Farming near George, Washington, 1975

It was a town you'd never
return to if you had
the ill star of ending
up there for god knows what.
I was there for potatoes,
camped by a rusty, half-sunk
trash can of a Quonset hut
and up each day at four
to torture my lips
with coffee boiled to mud
in a ten cent pot
from the Salvation Army
and spiked with hooch
to get us through the day.
One gas station, two bars,
and Rosy's Cafe was just about it.
At Joe's Club you could hear
the farmhands jaw through
their tractor dirt for hours
and hours about the tits
of some waitress or who
was dinking the sheriff's wife.
You were listening to
America's heartbeat, I guess,
after thirteen hours riding
the harvester, throwing the cow bones
and blight-sick milky hulks
of potatoes into the trashed fields,
the digger beneath you loud
as a B-52. Rosy's was the place

where you'd tabasco your hash-browns
week after week finding the same
farmhands jawing, jawing
till you walked out the door
and ran into the morning
that lit up the highway
from Spokane to Yakima
in a way you never noticed
from your place on the diggers,
no bonus if you quit.
So Rosy's it was and always
would be—the sky bright
all the way to the Rockies, crisp
as a French fry, golden as heaven,
there for you here, now.

Cutting Cedar Shakes in the Aladdin Star Valley, 1975

Deep in winter the work went on—
the knock of mallet on the froe
into the top inch of wood, then the twist
and pop as the shake sang off

and span to the ground, or, caught by hand,
was passed into the pile.
The other parts—the bark, the culls,
boards too curved by knots for use—
went to the other pile
that slowly heaped in the driveway
on the ice until the cold
of the work, the height of the wood,

or some deep love of flame
called for the can
of gasoline.

With a quick dowse and a tossed lit match,
the pyre rose high in burning.

It was afternoon then,
and all the day of work
was measured by the waste we lit
and stood before, warming,
cold beers in hand
to signal the end of something—
the day, a shake pile, all our labor.

Even as we stood, the heat
worked into the driveway ice.
It sent small rivulets of water
running down the driveway

toward the road, sometimes freezing,
sometimes reaching
the Star Route.

Harvest

In the places where we walked
homesteaders had once tilled
acreage; but since then
more than a century has gone.
All that remains of their breaking
of the earth are the mossy
underlogs of barns and houses
long since dissipated
in the hunger of moss and fungus.
About them stand the apple trees,
feral, climbing still
among the larch and aspen.

Each tree has turned its fruit
away from commonalities
of produce to the subtle
adaptive accidents
of difference in tartness, sweetness,
taste, size, shape; distinct,
shrunken, varicolored
      —again
the great introspection

of nature; again
the grace notes of mutation,

fruit and sweetness drifting toward
the coming wilderness.

Apples, cannabis, and insects.
Apple-gorged and smoked out,
we would sit and listen
as the humming, sexual waves
of insects worked across the fields,
opening with the moving of
the songs, each indistinct, all mixing
into one great rhythm.
These too came in swells
as each species was fulfilled,
its sound replaced in surges rolling
over us as we sat,

listening, tasting: here to know
some part of the world: the fruit, the harvest.

Goats

—*near Northport, Washington, 1974*

A goat full of Camel Cigarette butts
is a wormed goat, people said. They carried
stumped out cigarettes in their pockets
and fed them to goats like kids giving sugar
to horses. The goats would eat them the way
they seemed to eat anything they could love,
which was everything. But Camel butts
weren't their only door to the human;

dinner slops mixed with ash tray fillings,
marijuana roaches, burnt hash-pipe foil,
everybody's chewing gum: anything's food
to a goat. And in other ways

they would cross that fickle line
we claimed as a boundary.
Unsuspecting foils of jealousy
learned a lot, or at least earned a limp,
from butting horns that showed who had
the cojones *this* side of the wire. One day
we took the trash to the Northport dump.
Two things were open, or opened; the gate
to the goat pen, and the door to the house.
When we came back the goats were lying
on the sofa they were eating;
the towels were gone; one was mounting the stove
while another nudged cupboard doors
for the cereal. Tiny goat turds
lay on the carpet like counters in some
unfinished game you could only play

if you saw through those weird, rectangular
coffin-lid pupils in the eyes of a goat
gone over into our world. We got them
out of the house, established some sense

of order, or at least what we thought
was hierarchy. Outside, the goats
nuzzled each other, gently opening
doorways to another life.

Burning the Gas

This evening the Kingdom of Heaven has come to earth
On Route Eighty-Four just east of Portland, Oregon.
Bach's B-Minor Mass is playing on the stereo.
I drive into the city under a flame

of indescribable sunset, and all around me
the buildings start to blaze with constellations,
each light a jewel in the electric necklace
of comfort, warmth, and wonder.

                              Suddenly
I see the Kingdom of Heaven; I understand
how all of this could be the afterbirth
of the quick flash across the infinite sky,
exploding in the gas cloud out of nothing

before the congelation of the stars
to cool ferocity. The road careens
with headlights dancing past like asteroids
or atoms tracking their determined paths

along the film pan of the cyclotron.
Coming down Columbia, toward the Pacific,
I'm turning south, bound for California,
in the general direction of the equator,

the point of maximum spin. I sit enthroned
in plastic, encased in steel; I burn
and breathe petroleum. Everywhere I free
molecular frenzy, loosen the unabated

joyous cellular dream division of cancer,
anarchic representations. I swerve and spin,
I see the magic gleaming of the city
spreading beyond the ramparts of the freeway

that bends its massive shoulder over the river,
in mad, expressionist drama, form and shadow,
light and power. Caroming and veering,
I dance my way through the Nintendo of heaven,

past light and noise, the steel and concrete barriers,
then shoot south on the highway into the dark.

Stars

How long it has been since with my axe
I staked out the familiar ground:
there the larch and tamarack bolts,
before me the marred stump, all the splinters
of my work in the cold earth
where I chopped wood for the cook stove.
I'd heft the axe in one hand, a bolt
in the other, measure by eye
the grains and fractures of the wood
then flip the bolt upright, long side up,
and step back even as the stillness
filled me, bring the axe up,
one hand sliding along the shaft
to give speed and grace. The blade came
easily across the years
that parted as the wood popped
under the blade, the anonymous trees
halved, split, kindled.
                                     At night, coming
home from a party, the sky above
muffled with the next big snow,
the lights of my car would plunge down the dark
just for a second as I turned in
the drive, and graze across the bolt
I left on the stump where the axe was jammed.
Nothing shone but the clear, brief stars
of sap that eased from the unseamed rings
of green wood, small tears of amber. Quickly
they were gone as the headlights swung
across the porch. I killed the engine.
Inside fire slept, waiting for fuel.

from

Departures

Childhood near Hollywood

Every day above us
the sun languished, lazing its way
across the sky like some skimpy
bikini-clad model on a tire.

We pictured sunglasses on the sun
to let it keep its glare to itself

but even then we suspected
its need to drink in sustenance
and so drew a stream
between sun and ocean
then hooted with laughter
as children do
and drew sex organs on the sun

then in a frenzy my little brother
scribbled across everything

and yelled out, "Los Angeles!"
The room filled with the screaming clutter

of every street corner god or huckster.
By now we were mad.
We were running around
tearing up pictures: the sun and moon
we had been drawing that afternoon

when my brother yelled "cut!"
and we started with scissors
along the curtains
and then the veneer
of the antique Italian desk. Left alone

we children were terrors, and would not atone
for our actions, or acting.

It all had to end when mother called.

We went out and piled in the station wagon,
leaving our small disaster.
When evening approached, waving flags of surrender,
we grew up and left,
yet still the sea

surrenders its life up to a sun
that boils each heaven to a bone.

Piers

The wastages and way stations of the ocean
take the coast in small denominations.
POP, a tropical island themed park
where at the end, in a semblance of volcano,
we'd ride small train cars out over the water,
has washed away, its wreckage clearly rendered
in the surfing scenes of *Lords of Dogtown*.
The pier at Santa Monica, more stable
perhaps, or calling for a deeper investment
for its boat moors, has since gone all touristic.
No more is it just a place to catch fish
with carny stalls and a famous carrousel.
At one time I would find the hidden niches
to cast my line from, pulling up small bass
and a few other fry, but I was no fisherman,
and never stomached gutting as well as I could.
At pier's end the boats unloaded their catch,
freight carts of fish kept chilled with blocks of ice,
on second-layer levels by the boat house.
Below the pier, amongst the staggered pylons,
druggies and queers rendezvoused. But what did I know
then of this? The few times fishing, the thousand walks
along the pier to its facing toward the water
then back, brings back to mind all I remember
of life along the ancient palisade,
the disappearing city of my youth.
Beside the California Avenue incline
the ruins of an old hotel, ornamented
in grand Egyptian frippery, had left
only the imprint of its swimming pool,
a large terra cotta colored basin
filled with the glyphs of Isis and Osiris,

and home to rubble and old shopping carts
pushed from the cliffs above in delinquent joy.
As Jeffers says, in the few thousand years
that sees the decimation of all cities
perhaps a few cascades of stone will linger,
signs of the more important monuments
of *homo fiduciarius*. But still
will stay the overall layout of the coast,
the eating ocean, solid in its ambivalence,
forever taking and depositing,
and rendering the rhythms of the coast
in the continuous music of its washing
as wave hits shore and pylon, carrying all
with its incessant beat: wave, wave, wave, wave.

Visiting Grandmother

I'd sit beneath the Italianate cabinet,
flicking the hanging handles of the drawers—

each one a flowered loop and tit
with an arabesque piercing of brass. I could handle

this fascination, thoughtless metallic
working;
      clack, clack, they sang on antique plackets

joined to the cherry dark wood. The pitches
differed, one a half-tone higher.

My grandmother, in lace frock and black, tight necklace
with a small cameo at the front,

said that I looked like Troy Donahue.
She was speaking to my father.

He had brought me, kid-blonde and awkward,
down coast to see her in her beachside apartment

filled with the burnish of her life.
She was passing out of existence.

    Driving home,
safe on the back seat
of the Plymouth coupe,

the tires humming on the scored coastal road,
I would start to enter the world of sleep
that keeps pitching back on itself,

      where dream
and waking become the same. My grandmother,
pale as the small ghost housed in the cameo egg at her
throat,

would speak to me
of the dreams of the world that we all are leaving,

that cannot be explained. I was riding
up to the coast on a wave as Troy Donahue
might surf his way to another beginning
TV series. This was the shape

of consciousness. Her smile grew red
with lipstick, her chin forming a canyon
of cracked, ridged flesh that was now easing
into the brooch, and the pink-pale face

of the cameo kept on looking sideways
into an even more distant world.

Flight

—for my father

It is again as it is
in the places that I have left
before night falls, and I sit
in the configuration
of stars and the lights of aircraft passing
away from the city into the blue
and blackening sky that stretches farther
than I have ever given thought
to wander. My father, hand
on the back porch railing,
wants it to be as it is;
I can see him looking
into the deepening well
of darkness. I can see
the way his fingers fidget
along the cool, black iron
of the banister.
If he could speak, I know
he would mention the chance
that summer could be here,
that we could be coming home
to sit together again.
I know he would be looking
for a way to tell me
that he is happy or sorry
for everything, for the way
night brings its dark wing
over us, and the distant lights
of aircraft blink down
to the orange edge of the day
that is quietly dying

into the black of the sea.
He would like to think of the way
an aircraft becomes a star,
filled with the luck of horizons
until there is no going home.

Shell

The sea is always giving up on land.
It leaves reminders, bears the principal,
deposits interest; in this case, a shell
that long since winked away from life, enjambed

Its clever creature's wrinkle out of water
into some hard and horny house, away
from all that water carries in its pay
of particle and current. A strange mother,

The water gives and takes with equal ease.
But now the child who walks the fluent field
where sea and land advance their cache will yield
and reach into the flow, as if to seize

the rapid, foaming treasure of the waves,
but only to identify the shell
that pulls along like paper in a gale.
Feeling it, he moves into a glaze

of interest himself. For now a net
of shy investments binds him to this world
he silently invites, before the curled
reminder of the day is marked and set

in pocket with his other talismans.
He later will arrange them on his bed
as tokens to the moments that have led
the sliding encrustation beyond skin,

the assets that become him. For he builds
a shell from bits and pieces, brings himself
to bear resemblance to this secret gulf
of bonds and certifiers of the wilds

he walks beside. And thus, by giving sense
to life, a self, a shell, he comes to live
by check and balance, counting on what gives
him chance to ebb into this difference.

Octopus

Under rocks washed with tides,
we children would sometimes find
a soft, chameleon octopus,
tentacled up and exaggerated
in its whisper of something
as close as life in the sea permits;
low oxygen levels
bearing on everything we call thoughts
or feelings, carrying all
about on its own in this different world,
water, with what we would call
deep reds of intention
flushing over the body, or cool
cucumber greens of solitude
considering what to do next,
this sly aquatic cat:

three hearts pump the copper-based
blood through the slow, lovely
push-push of sex and death.
Increasingly complex,
the octopus calculates all,
rehearses the imperative
for distant, landed cousins.
For the sea starves off the need to skim
objectively after tasks or things;
what is, floats by: the copulant,
the lounger, dinner, registered
in this reduced activity.
Strange bedfellow, the octopus:
waiting for lunch to catch up,
spreading the egg or seed just once,

then dying; sending off a ghost
of him-slash-herself, and so escaping
everything, wailing away
with eight legs through the water, leaving
a phony reference—completely disjointed,
the predators fooled by ink;
it slinks to the deep, slime soft, slippery,
this sly aquatic body.

Gone Too Far near Singing

The way light may weigh on sense
or seal the gesture of the land,

or how a scene may slip in sunset
into pools of gestures;

these are words where afternoons
can read their presence into night.

They say how songs can captivate
a landscape; worlds of dragonflies

then weave between the undulations
of the cattails raised from water

now in how it all retrieves us.
Then we see too closely in

the world to get away. Thought ends.
We find ourselves

gone too far near singing not
to be the sound of breath.

Departures

Picture the wicker of the rippled water
as he remembers it, or recall
the surface burnished smooth as stone, the weather
easy as a summer ought to be;
easy as the liquor in the glass
through which the table's curvature distorts
into a bulging eye, or else an egg
forever unbroken. After it passes the lip,
the loud song of vodka in the mouth
details another moment of departure,
another salutation to the missing
that brings him back across the continent
to face again the place where waves slap down
and splash the land below the orange-brown cliffs
he'd climb down to reach the sea and find her
mottled in foam and in memoranda of driftwood,
in the Hottentot fig and coastal flowers
that open spiked heads outward toward water.
On the bicycle path he'd follow homeward
past the fields where deer feed in wild wheat,
the black heads of grasses sway in breezes
before you and behind you. If you remember
the waves of grass, if you recall the sound
of birds as they chirp their hopelessness,
if you recall the seed of loss that opened
in his voice, the dream of the second person,
then you know the time is ripe for departure,
for the land between us is as real
as the brief stretch of my hand before my eye,
and yet as ineffaceable as stone,
as insistent as the patterning of water,
and as hard as the broken love that comes between us.

from

Contingencies

Extinction

—for Robinson Jeffers

From the tower he had built the poet
looked out on contingencies of oceans
and words, and reached through whiskey
and cigarettes toward understanding.
He was not far from the scene of disaster,
his and ours, and the underlying crystallized
fetish he drew from visions served
the way a careful teller is served
by spreading and backdating lending to hide
the paying out of small denominations,
a dry poem or a type of toad, the forests
turned into houses, tides of roads, the heavy
and overburdened atmosphere.
All need just be observable, reported,
leaned in on, as if one were at the banister
looking into the circles of hell
toward the great frozen lake, but instead
it was waving, the tightness gone out of it,
a loose death. The wave was advancing,
a committee was reporting on extinctions,
warning of consequences from loss of species,
labeling what was called a way of life
as the culprit in demise.
And he watched it, sometimes conjuring
over a bowl of blood or a stone
as a prop in composing, watched the ways
death would fly in the room, as quiet
as a cat or a fog, come, vanish all,
lead into it, the nothingness of not
knowing, beyond the frame of every end
that would not change. The blood drained;

annihilation, nihilism,
each moment gleaming and crushed
as if by rigid stone, the social order spinning
into final chaotic survivalist
impulse, cracking the nut open, letting
the skull of the world ripple pointless
dreams of possession into phantom
realities, even as the end blossomed
in his thought. Courage is not
in the air at such times, he thought, but requires
continuing into the light, recognizing
that it all teeters on the brink and shall
continue teetering, contingent, though thought
resist all that announces any
awareness of how it leans to collapse:
recognize, accept, understand at least once:
love our demise as we learn to foresee it.

Grape Cluster

the gape of the art
of the gold green turning
leaves in the cluster
the dense texture
of webbed cob
and spider hiding
in purple
cleavages
of grapes

waiting for taste
some kiss of sun
out of mist
its own web
hanging over the valley

an accident of light
echoing grey hair

succulent
or very real
spider
calculation

to be alive
each chance incident
in the vineyard
a dancing

Heard Singing

The lone bird
keeps returning
to the tree
to sing in the hot night

a different bird
each time
yet the same sense
pervades the calling

the same tree
and limb
the same spirit
moving them

and I know
of what I hear
that this and
every moment

is the only moment

a hot night clings to.

Matilde

—*after Neruda*

Matilde—name of plant, or stone,
or wine, or what is known of the earth,
endures; a word which the morning crescendos
infused with the light of lemons.
                    Within
this name
the wooden ships
are sailing,
rounded enjambments
of the sea-blued firs.
The letters ride the river waters,
descanting through the heart.

Name unencumbered under tangling,
like the door to an unknown tunnel
that leads to the fragrances of the world!

Invade me with your hot mouth! Uncover me
with night-dark eyes.

Let me navigate, sleep in your name.

Wild Solo

It blew wild, and the will welled
so low into the solidity
of the solace

the welkin welcomed the wished child
so the law could walk

it being every abandoned low solo
sung so low he saw what
was sewn
                    wheat,
the white wit of the clever
he saw sung so sewn, whetted
wink of the luring aces

each wild solo of the sax
brought back the relaxed enhancement
of the trashed out tenement

the word carried the corpse of the idea
into extravagance

also in spite of the spittle dribbled
occasionally into the instrument

he played this way, paid against death,
the pawed alternative possible
no more contingent than the operation

the band played on

Contingencies

Here is everything she said about coming to America:
        chrome airport railings, reflected glares
        of neon, traffic dizzying the terminal.

She spoke of Rastafarians roomed with during those first
few weeks;
        bundled marijuana hanging like mistletoe
        in the apartment.
                                        She had come
        to study the culture of San Francisco,
wound up in a loose suburb,
missed all sense of what she was seeking.
        Couldn't concentrate. Decided to stay.

Outside, jackhammers
keep pulverizing
the street. They have
to go out.
He wants Chinese; she says pizza.
A car passes. She thinks something's
incomplete: cities with no center.
Wonders what he thinks. His mind careens,
a fast car skidding on a thin road
        near the edge like it did
                in the movie.

                        May nothing
ever be reconsidered:

the cops knocking, complaints about barking
dogs; they missed the pot. These things
would happen when you arrived. Walk the streets.

See how the homeless sleep in newspapers.
Someone plays blues harmonica
outside a drug store. Like any city
with its destitute and insane,
    no design behind the skin
      clinging
           to the whispers beneath,
               in some way it all fit
                  the life;

enter the right places, lights and noise stun you;
drinks, décolletés, spasmed thrashings in strobe lights.
It was intended like this;

we each might have stood, coat conspicuously
slung off a shoulder, wanting to approach
some special someone while the floor shimmered
and outside the city lifted its gold throat
    to storms
           as it might
the second you let
the needle go
and the stuff hits—freight train
so fast on the john you laugh eyes closed
body gone, faces beyond description,
empty heart jumping. It all eludes you:
pass the project on to others;
    dealers in everyday occupations,
    drugs meaning little beyond a meal

in some circles, fitting into the ventured
program at Capital's heart.
    Didn't such dreams spawn empires and fortune?

Hadn't it brought islands into the culture?

Contingency;
        what occurs
                after the fact of the accident.

Pacific Standard Life Insurance, for instance:
first a facade, then broad green lawns
reaching the street. Each lawn rises
into a mound or battlement
reminiscent of the barrows left
by the Saxons or Cherokees
for their important dead. Each descends
to the "exterior," as the committee
calls it at meetings—
                     benches and tables,

cool green grass. Above, a trellis:
grape and ivy intertwine

and filter light, so that, at lunch,
or if luck or power give you an office
facing out, you have floating purity
of the light in partial rainbows
on the interest, tints, expectancies
captured in figures, clarifying chance,
defining risk. Such dancing flights

        of thought:
light refracted across a desk.

from

In a Window

War Is Opened

It happens like this almost every time.
One thing, another; descent into reverie
after the panic. Train cars break up
in the slow-motion sun-colored ochre
under standards that defy the brightness
of logic. "War is opened," the headlines read.

Meanwhile, the ebullience of litter
spills from cardboard in every garbaged
bog of alley, and the electric
neon nervosity of it rings
the paths of felines that seek understanding
or at least discarded heads of fish.

In these messages bearing the mess
of post-deconstruction, any Burning Bush
is God. Then the mailman discounts
the whom on the brick-curbed, weather-stained letter
from all that can be granted to power
or at least the firmness of the cigarette.

War is opened on grammaticity,
sign of the times, the cleanly concocted
and clearly depersonalized zone of the poet,
as if all advertisement were schmaltz
instead of negation of the unwanted.
Was there a square bit of form shining forth?

Define it by number. Hence a logic
of meter, the scantron of art we can under-
take or at least -stand, since declaration
defines us and anyway here we are
with cats that at least know what they're after
among the backdoor discardings of flowers.

In a Window

a bird cuts down like a needle
a needle of bird
    across the fabric of trees

water cross-stitches
one elm bucks like a horse in the wind
behind it, others,
more serene, only sway lightly,

dignified, two parents
overlooking a child
    the dripping juniper
with earrings of rain
occupies an intense forest
    trees lean together, kiss
        incest
two fingers of them reach
    toward the window, across the walk

they have spent their life reaching

    but the wind
    knows how to move them
in secret ways that for them are dreams
baptism and subtle marriages
the unknown quantity
the sinuous curve of resistance
being blown
springing back

the zipper of wet tires on road
an occasional plane beating the air
and everywhere continuing commentary

      birds chirp repeatedly
      as if urgent
      a conversation in a restaurant

one streaks in with a glorious insect
         the moist air
the slicing crystals of rain
a gutter drips bamboo music
thirds and tonics repeated
I see in the window, faintly
      my reflection
a big blue target of shirt
reflecting against green trees
      and gray sky

Evening Conversation

—for Robert Penn Warren

Reckless and white as a flashlight beam cast
into some dark corner, the moon
insists on the deeper blackness

surrounding it. Perhaps it wishes
to be a woman or a window,
outshining everything, full of itself

for the moment, yet frightened, like any egotist.
But still the stars patiently insist
on their presence, pinholes to nothingness.

When else would I walk on such a night in the world?

Half answers suggest themselves.
The body consumes and wanes, collapses.
We get to watch how everyone
dies who dies before us,
how birds rest.

And yet while night solidifies,
we can continue our discussion
in our effort to open the gift of the world,
our hope to find years
in this box we tear apart.

Birds do not count in our calibration.
They crack time randomly, as if it were seeds.
With sudden unaccountability
they start up and disappear.

And yet, in some way all of this
is beside the point, for what can we do
except continue our conversation,
and what would we gain if we disappeared?

They tell us that this is so.

Do you have any songs from your childhood
you still use to sing yourself to sleep?

Being, mind, ego: the moon loves itself
in cloud shimmers, dancing as if it had pulled
a scant nightie off a laundry line
to clown with.

We can only walk while there is light.

Entering Strange Cities

"The erection itself is not incompatible with the system"
—Jean Baudrillard

Entering the strange cities,
one finds the trees that are reaching up like supplicating hands,
or only like the branches that grow toward the light from beyond
the world.

Or else there are no trees;
the lights of the city drone over empty streets like homeless bees.
Emaciated figurines reach up to catch the baseballs of light.
Or else there is no light. The buildings are dark, their strata
founder in rows of windows, or the sides of the factories
pound, or in suburbs
cities are named and hum
as images on television sets, cities are dreamed of as if they too
were real, for
to use the tongue
to scent a path
through ideas
requires signs,
and these, significant
or other, call forth
the glottal,
rituals of slobber,

the waves the eye sees as water
edging up or moving through the city in incandescence.

This is the central monument: the carved statue of the hero;
under it, the child, a part of no statue, addicted, falling apart.
In other places the mutant man is moving—

look onto the streets of any city where trees lift like hands,
or only as trees;

look where the loosened suitcase flops on the sidewalk in
the small disasters of the tourist; look where someone wears
eyeglasses as thick as porcelain, wide eyed; in the swimming
shift of light each hand is reaching toward a different end.
The chameleon line of the blinded eye strikes as he reads the
braille book, one hand moving across the page in English,
one in Arabic, and the book ripples, its thick pages wattled
like turkey skin, three fingers flying one way, one the other, and
the sense of it all in the touches nonchalantly bent, a birdlike
flight of the hand entering the strange city in an unfamiliar way,

by vehicle or path, for each road separates how one is approached in
cities as much as how one approaches. One finds the trees that are
rising
like supplicating hands,

or else one only finds the trees that still are lifting branches
toward the light from beyond the world. Or else one finds
no trees,
for some cities
work to topple trees,
to bring the freedom no tree brings,
the high, cracked love of buildings;

the factory of winds that move fiercely
across the frozen lands.

Hard

A hard gray, the lake has entangled the skies—
gulls, winds, waves, clouds—
this face of wrath too windy to read,
the rain not yet born.

This is how it is in moments
when it becomes clear what you will not do.
Death wears a similar face to weather—
obstructive, constant, fickle.
A wind turned on and off.

The sun continues beyond these clouds
unconnected to hope
except in the way a rolling coin
joins to effects of sidewalks—
cracks and imperfections denying
distance.

                    Things simplify—
eating, breathing, taking a walk,
tying a shoe—

the weather widens

the waves hit the shore,
angry pillows of water
slapped on a bed

in the dazed moments before some sleep.

Meditation on Bliss

"Why write about bliss? There's a war on!"

War was invented by the flowers,
as the English and Aztec knew.
Lavenders attacked jacarandas
with luscious scents and iodine.
Soon the rhododendrons learned
to poison the earth by opening blossoming
empires of color. The bees made golden
by pollen produced the honey that drove
the foraging Macedonians mad
in Alexander's campaign.
Then petals fell in legion;
soon there were just the endless acts
of blossoming holding the flowery world
together.
               Bliss exists outside
of time; it lives in eternal moments
inside and outside of war. It knows
the bloom of dust borne up by the bullet
that misses its mark, and leaps in joy
as the target stumbles beyond the sights.
It is one and is always winning.
It only demands complete surrender.

The Eater of Avocados

Opening

The militant leaves try to disguise them
in small memos of jungle.
He is too clever; he brings ladders.
Reaching up, he finds them;
thumbs of another substance, coarse
and gangly, too awkward to twaddle.
Their freeing is easy, a twist, a technique.
With practice it comes to nothing.

As the knife easily passes
through the skin the fruit surrenders.
He opens the soft, lopsided round
to find the green sky,
a teardrop of taste
coddled in oily atmospheres
along the curved horizon:
                                    sunrise!
The yellow illumes the hard and pithy
redolent football seed:

the tree is waiting
to get cracking.

Eating

It brings forth the first word
in the alphabet of taste.
Soft with water and southern dust,
it calls for salt and lemon;
the red ghosts of powdered chilies
flavor the syllabation: *AH!*
shape of the tongue and mouth
that shy and round to the form of fruit,
a small, green, leather-cassocked monk
who advocates sensation: *VO!*
the oiled variations on
a theme that gleams on chins, greens teeth,
receives these flavors speaking of
the ease of eating: *CA!*
a crow's weight of fruit in trees
with spatula leafs; the spiced scent
of the orchards through which deer move:
DO! philosopher of flavor,
Dogen, eminent Buddha,
jade or emerald, purchase of price—
rough alligator texture
of the throwaway skin.

Discarding

Round
of the green sky
thickens inside,
solidifies
with a soiled
atmosphere:

this fruit:
seed within
a planet swimming
in oil:

this then
is the secret
of the avocado:

Things to be done, things to be done, the world at large
resting as if under the too heavy necessity of change,
as if the weight of contradiction were bearing down like a
large crack; and then the smokiness enters the taste,
and then comes the slow loss
of softness in
these hard black fibers

Pound to Joyce

Suppose you moved to Zürich for a year;
would you have minded making your own furniture?

Perhaps you would have put up in a town
beside the lake. Suppose your real fear

had not been want of lodging or the war,
but here; a letter sent without the cheque

as I had promised; how money seems to queer
its way in everything.
                            Suppose the boot
of some pig prince were given you, and you
could ask him to rise up and give the world

its truest art. Think of the ease with which
you would have laughed while flags unfurled the end

of all that mocks us: wealth and grace, the power
and the glory in your face.
                            Joyce, I wanted
to make everything, from furniture
to paradise, and still the music, slow and lean,

burned just beyond my fingers while I killed
the tale within,
                            and all my thoughts of passion

and its necessary erasure,
having slain the beast that eats our stories,
ran in terror from the gash. We thrill
to see a future as long as we are in it.

One can kill the piper later. In all,
I leave you just this melody of jackboots.

Ulysses sailed without a port at hand.

In Memory of Abbie Hoffman

1

One of them is casual, cool, smirking into his hand.
The other rests, fully clothed, in bed.
One is figuring out how to cause all the garbage cans
    in the city to ignite at once.
One is tired of computer consultants.
One faces crowds from atop a statue,
    wearing underwear and chanting in Urdu.
One (rumor has it) eats the shit
    of Frank Zappa on stage, live
    from New York, thereby winning the gross out.
One knows the whole shebang has collapsed,
    the years of hiding from the F.B.I. only mean a new face.

2

This poem has been set to explode.
It contains at least seventy percent
of the alphabet. Cut this poem up.
Rearrange the letters. For instance,
"settler" or "settle" becomes a possibility
if you are quick. If not, this poem
is set to explode. Draw a line
down the poem, apply X-Acto knife:
you now have "explode
        y percent
        oem up
        instance," et cetera, for instance;
you have saved this poem. You now can see
how to disarm it. Be careful.

3

Abbie, Abbie, Abbie,
knowing all the things we do
to make a point, clarify
an idea, personal, political—
on trial in Chicago, you ate it,
and later
running from the law
changed your face
so you could surface
in various odd positions.

Fully clothed, dead in bed,
done on drugs, stiffing up,
your name stays yet in my mind
as a kind of yo-yo, a way to disgrace
that graces simultaneously;
insult or accident, joke or malignance,
the total reversion
to overturn of order
calls up the permanent
revolution
just for the hell of it;

you, like me, *frère, hypocrite lecteur,*
if at all you do remember
the need of disorder, the casting of chaos
in the arena just to confound
the sentiments of the latent death squads
bear in mind
the heart of the matter
yippie to yuppie, think it over
and if you remember, tear the page
from the book. Steal this poem.

Waitress

She has spent all these years getting mad at the main course,
dancing her fear in and out through the door—

the sad chocolate cream pies, the plates of French fries,
quickly side-arming as she twists down in front

of the guy whose cigarette floats in his leftover
coffee: the thing she's dying for;

her own escape, break: the alcove between
the kitchen and the room where heads plunge toward food

lifted up on old forks—cigarettes, gin,
the nightly valium bearing her off to sleep:

away from the daily bread she gives up
out of boredom or pain: Disney white cape

and apron over the orangish, muddy
dress, earth-brown like a deep muck one finds

in rich scoops of back-washed swamps
where dead fill gathers and sinks, heats, compacts
into rich soil:
                              the dress, these careworn
hands, nails hot scarlet over

the chipped and bitten reality
and the nicotine stains: the lip-sticked swishes
of lack of considering anything
like you human or worth the time
but only a passing check, a quick buck—

if there were some way of making it,
she would not be here, not leaving
butts afloat in the Styrofoam take-out
coffee-cup ashtray she takes outside

when it's too much. She needs to be free
the time it takes to suck up the blue

and poisonous cigarette smoke under
the neon lights that erase the stars.

Return

Leaving Phoenix

Clouds sweep over the fuselage,
pass and wave like grasping hands.
Farther from the jet they hang,
dense and empty mountains,
freezing air and water. As

      we move
the sweet
geometry
of streets and corners
glides into
dry scrabble. Stone and desert
below us stretch in all directions.
The air outside would kill us not through malice,
only by its thinness.

This is the way the earth will part with us:
not just through the ancient light on stone,
but with the thirsting of the invented suck,
the vacuum pulling our fleet tons of steel
through the narrow clinging of the air
to earth in small, contingent waves we jet through.
What life awaits? What is the new direction?
Behind us, Phoenix, our point of connection,
rises like its eponym, a bird
that rose from its own ashes, and yet there
life rises from bare dirt, a concrete dream,
a banked and careful manufacturing
of all desire and all imagination.

I sit, flying, following sunlight. I read
about the Jews and their predestination,
and then about Japan, and biologicals
they tested secretly in World War Two.
The sun I fly to will soon rise for them
in their reborn economy beyond
the west I witness from this shining craft
that hones its path of emptiness from sky.

Climbing Blue Canyon, Lake Berryessa, California

I have always
already dreamed
myself in this air
left long ago:

not for its taste
of hills and fires,
but for how
it is not disturbed
by the breeze
that licks down
like a tragic tongue,
causing a tingle on the skin,
over lips,
taking speech.
One here only knows heat.

Silence hangs in everything;
all that matters is to continue
moving upslope. A bird is landing;
rock, scrub brush,
flowers, sage,
dog's ear. Now a vulture

is working long, loose looping cyphers:
writes and erases, writes and erases

across the sky, zeros, haloes,
suspending nothing

it does not mean. An oak leaf
wags upon a tree.

Climbing, we do not speak. Nothing
moves but
with heat,

a breeze shimmering golden grass,
dead grains awaiting fire or water.

Old Town: Davis, California

This is the way the towns you leave
will leave you: leaving every street
the same, inchoate, while all heartaches
visit someone else
and all the promises and hopes
you left with meet at the edge of town
like dogs after any sign
of your return or leaving,
after anything to bark at,
as if this life were not yet enough.

So look around. The streets
gleam with clarity,
the dust and the cafes remain the same;
a building somewhere goes up or comes down,
a tree declines or blossoms,

and the fields continue bathing
in the pall of heat, the face
of nothing, unperturbed, unusual,
still, distinct. Coming from
the air, you realize how every dream
has left you, how every situation
lingers on in indecision.
You could turn back now
and walk along these streets
in unforgetting,
since all that's here has long
forgotten you. Each hope
dies in gardens bright with flowers,
and angelic lights of disappointment
everywhere direct their ashes toward you
until you must admit that you are here,
which means that you have to give up

and recognize what all this is:
a town, not one you left
or one that you return to,
but just a genuflection
to dwelling.
Everything
carries on
in life.
It lives in itself, and so projects you.
You come back to find it, confused,
amazed, detached, unreal, and yet still here.

Stephenson Bridge Road

—near Davis, California

The Coast Ranges are burning.
Nut brown plumes of brush fire
rise to north and west.
To the east, invisible,
the Sierra Nevada
are marked by wads of thunderhead.
In the valley, between fire
and rain, the world is different—
dreamy, green and yellow,
hot with the snap-dry air.

As we bicycle,
we turn south on the road
to Stephenson Bridge—
tough WPA work
spanning Putah Creek.
Over the years graffiti—
faces, pictures, signs—
have spread across it—
angled, illegible words;
strange, random sloshes
of color on concrete,
making this place a stony
throwback to the sixties.
The bridge almost seems
to outshine the bright,
flowing zucchini field
bursting with golden flowers
where the road angles in:
sharp, dangerous curves,
swastika-like beside

the bank, a deep, depressing
purple spilled down pillars
to the creek: car parts. Tires.
Cans. A clear jar.
All the relentless trash
of humanity
on the creek bank and roadside,
and above, the bridge:
the gang signs, the sexual
boasting, sworn endless love
in a homogeny
of delirious colors,
all these shades and juices
so intently rendered:

    the names flow
    mad and sensual
    color explosions
    interwoven

erasing each other against horizons
marked by smoke and clouds.

Listening to Buddhists While Driving into Nevada

The highway leads us to the golden promise.
It moves toward the stars, past Desolation,
the Wilderness Area clinging in grey-white
rocky prominence above us, granite
massed over the forest. But halfway there
half the forest has burned completely over.
This is the road that leads to the casinos.

This is the road under "improvement." We wait
half an hour as the Russ Food Vans
pass the washout while the workers smoke
their cigarettes. We put in a tape
of mountain people, tantric Buddhist monks,
chased out of their homeland, now living in Berkeley.
Underneath the burn a few bright elms
have come back among the tamaracks.

The stars
slowly grow
with the rise of night
on the west edge
of the continent as we wait
to drive into the state of games,
the monks chanting prayers on the stereo,
filling the world of the car, or filling
night or all the possible thoughts
of risk the billboards play upon,
showing the man who rolls out the dice
and shouts out "Oh, Baby!"
as the paneled truck goes by

following the flag car.
I turn on the motor,
momentarily cut the chant,
and we follow in the line
like ants entranced by pheromones.

At the crest sky opens in all directions,
empty of all meaning, full of hope.

Desolation

In their deepest interweave of chanting,
so it is said, the monks' deep basses cross
and recross in cascades of overtones
that hum and spin, and gradually take form
in the image of a dancing child,
or even as some geometric shape,
and this is Shiva dancing in the origin
and in the end enacted.

      As we drive
the energy keeps booming through the stereo,
and everything is already here
at the other edge of Desolation,
by Lake Tahoe.
      And yet, when we hike
into this place where man is not allowed
his work, we find the human everywhere,
not just where campers spread their neon tents,
but even on the trail we follow up

to the hard geometries of granite.
The maps and signs tell us where we are heading,
and names have been attached to every peak.
We follow trail blazes, count the time
to get in, go up, and get out again,
to reach the car by nightfall. At Velma Lakes,
even the ducks are tuned in to our game;
they recognize the presence of the beast

that feeds them. One swims to us on the shore,
walks out, waits for food, then scratches, jumps
back in the water, bored with all that ogling
that doesn't bring a handout. Silence reigns;

plants go on with growing, slow explosions
out of the form we place on all we touch.
They are intent only on the water
and sunlight moving on these slopes in summer.

Tahoe City

Along the roadside, buildings cluster:
restaurants, stores, and hotels;
bicycle rentals and accessory shops.
     This is a tourists town,
and we are tourists here, not here for casinos
or jet skis, just for the woods, air, water,
trees and animals, life.

     Down south, someone
also seeks his pleasure in the woods.
He's lit nine forest fires in two days,
then disappeared, leaving the smoke haze
that blots camera views and scenes of the lake
from the slopes.
     We're here for the scene;
scene, not the action, action, not interaction;
only the way up and down,

     in and out
of these ancient mountains; this is what we are here for.

Coming out of the Wilderness,
one finds lines of cars
crawling from California.
These are places we have invaded:
sailboats, jet skis, silences, impostures,
dildos, swordfish, hamburgers, a trolley.

Everything assigned an importance
in the cash crop of the tourists
flowing through by the millions
each year like spawning fish.
Here the water slowly bursts and sinks,

thousands of years. Board feet
of trees lie idle,
listless in noonday heat.

We look at forests
and see nothing.

Mt. Tallac

The forest is organization, deep and strong
It leaves its lilac scripture in the lichen
spreading up the schist. It knows the lesson
in the fracture lines of stone,
                    the explosion
up and out of ponderosa pine,
the extravagance of flowers. It spreads
dreams the way imagination
might spread were it not held
by the thought of all that
might be real or unreal.

        Call it self-unconsciousness, distraction;
the fact is the mountain is here,
shedding skin in talus slopes
we scramble on, climbing for hours
from the point where forest dwindles,
leaving traces only twisting
out of rocks like those of dreams

or the lush green leaf
with its Christmas spires of parasite.

Here a worm or caterpillar
blends onto a leaf. The ridge
it forms marks
the unity
of rocks,
                    the slope
of mountains, dust
we kick up with our feet
as we go up, come down, go on.
                    Later,

night is cool at camp, the stars are everywhere
silent between the trees. The quiet grows
from outside and inside. We see how
the dreaming evening passes into nothing
that is not joined to us. We find the stars
shining empty, airless light through space,
and somehow in the coolness we feel warm.

Tourists

On one side
                    the lake
        on the other
        the bar,
colored parasols,
        noise
rock music, laughing drinkers
boasting about accomplishments—
the enclosed world. Men in tee-shirts,
girls in chic dresses. Being here

is a statement. It shows wealth
and status. There is no being
other than this need
to understand the night
      with stars outside the lights
of entertainment.

        Next to us, quietly, suddenly,
a lake wave washes against the breakwater.
It is there. This is the way
water unveils itself

     not with a laugh
but with a ripple
      oxygenating,
         spreading simplicity
into the deepening pools of concentration,
into the rock it hides within itself.
It separates the mountains from each other,
makes pebbles round as teardrops on the beaches,
eroded form liberated in water:

leaf drip, blown splash, rock wave, plain of stillness
water laughs, and drinkers laugh
boast of sport or job, eye
each other, checking skirt length, comparing
compromising thoughts in liquid form,

     the bottle
       late at night. Shutting up.
Everyone has gone to bed
except one drunkard, lost in the sea
of his weaving, wary and slow,
close to unconsciousness.
A waiter helps him wash out of the door.

Beach

I am the lord of the stones. I am the water.
I am the landing goose. I am the gull.
Spiral of wave or bird that lands in water.
Thought of the person looking into the lake.

The lake here is cold. This is a harbor,
a house. Swimmers are allowed. The water
says nothing about swimmers. There are machines
to take care of everything.
                        The leaves.
The humid septic tanks just off the road.
This is the land of water and dry land.
This is the way of water. First, the feet
enter and freeze. The toes strike against rock.

Then water lifts to shins and thighs,
and one is safely in. When thoughts are water,
water is the magnitude of thought.
Thought takes the form of water. Then it flows

over the ideas and imaginings
that dart or sit upon the rocky bottom
called reality. This is where feet hurt.
Despite the numbing atmosphere of water,

this is the end of thinking as we know it:
breeze in the heat upon the shore, eyes closed,
ears wide, open to the world, all thought
gone. This is for a moment everything
that comes to life in water or in sunlight:
wave, light, heat, slight breeze, everything and nothing
being experienced until time has passed,
when we gather towels and head for home.

Red Duff

The granite pulverized to powder
                    rises
white-grey ash

across the trail
and down the whole
slope of
the mountain.

Here and there, trees have succeeded
in securing some support,
an isle
            of green
in the grey white talus.

One tree has fallen
to the parentheses of dust;

slowly it returns the sleep
of cells to the first powder,
plant to earth to mineral.

            The sun leaches water;
the soil is now a fine pattern of red,
a desert color.
                    Were one to look for water,
were one to look in this place
for anything resembling
or recalling private life
this alone would be found,
dust in dust
            differently colored.
Yet the sorrow of passing life

does not intrude.

                Come here
for what is freed
through the love of whirlwinds
of duff down
from fire. The dust
is slowly inverting
in spirit, and now
forming the dust devil, upside down,
in the shape of a cedar tree,

bringing all again to life
just in the moment of silent spin.

Range of Light

Onion Valley

The pinnacles of the sierra
lift up from here
to a sky

now graying with sunlight
and purple near
where water runs
down cliff sides

alpenglow orange upon stone

in the measure of everything
light holds pinnacles motionless
fading
the crag over us
like the home of some
unearthly goat
      light
everywhere alive
like the water
of Robinson Creek

running down a mountain

how can one help but be alive
how can one help but be moving toward dying

Object

a green lake in the scree
of granite above the glacier cut cliff
rounds like a punch bowl
a cirque, then lifts
to crags

on the water's surface
wind silently moves
the green breaks with flecks of light
these irreversible patterns:

the bow shape of wind swimming
across the lake continued in light
reflection   the moving fragmentation
of water's surface
near Kearsarge Pass
eleven thousand feet
in the air

Green, Gray, White, Blue, Brown

down the valley, silhouetted pines:
not up yet, the sun's light grows
smoky orange yellow wash and white line
only Venus remains
of the field of stars spread over us

I sit behind the quaking aspens
witnessing everything
part of the spectrum

In Camp

a butane camp lantern
flickers in the wind
forms a center
of night
a fire
        and a sense
of warmth
beyond what is watching
if anything
has eyes for us

"that which sees is truly seen"
the knower of its own seeing
or animal eyes
flash like yellow, paired stars

Dream

You wake once at night and say
"Look! a bowl of stars!" Then
later, your glasses on
you see there is only Venus
refracted
in your uncorrected
eyesight
        and yet
        protectress

Venus bowls us
over every
time

sun's guard
lucifer
shepherd's star
names legion
light one

Range of Light

— *Kearsarge Pass*

At some point everything falls away
into light: perhaps coming into
the pass, or when there is no place
higher to go without ascending
into the air.
      Light then occupies
everything: you, your lover, rocks, ice
the sky, the trees that ripple below

the point where life no longer is needed.

Rocks, ice, and sky are always enough
in the cycles of time that pivot
here. This is the source of forests:

this range of light forever ascending.

About the Author

Allan Johnston earned his M.A. in Creative Writing and his Ph.D. in English from the University of California, Davis. His poems have appeared in over sixty journals, including *Poetry, Poetry East, Rattle,* and *Rhino.* He has published two full-length poetry collections (*In a Window*, Shanti Arts, 2018; and *Tasks of Survival*, 1996) and three chapbooks (*Northport*, 2010; *Departures*, 2013; *Contingencies*, 2015). He has received an Illinois Arts Council Fellowship, Pushcart Prize nominations (2009 and 2016), and First Prize in Poetry in the Outrider Press Literary Anthology competition (2010). He teaches writing and literature at Columbia College and DePaul University in Chicago, and reads or has read as a contributing poetry editor for *Word River, r.kv.r.y,* and the Illinois Emerging Poets competition. He is also co-editor of *JPSE: Journal for the Philosophical Study of Education.* His scholarly articles have appeared in *Twentieth Century Literature, College Literature,* and several other journals.

SHANTI ARTS

NATURE · ART · SPIRIT

Please visit us online
to browse our entire book
catalog, including poetry
collections and fiction, books
on travel, nature, healing, art,
photography, and more.

Also take a look at our highly
regarded art and literary journal,
Still Point Arts Quarterly, which
may be downloaded for free.

WWW.SHANTIARTS.COM

www.ingramcontent.com/pod-product-compliance
Lightning Source LLC
Chambersburg PA
CBHW021505090426
42739CB00007B/480

* 9 7 8 1 9 5 6 0 5 6 5 3 2 *